A
Government
SECRET

Raúl Rodriguez

AquaZebra™
Book Publishing
Cathedral City, CA

This is a work of non-fiction. Unless otherwise noted, the author and the publisher make no explicit guarantees as to the accuracy of the information contained in this book and in some cases, names of people and places have been altered to protect their privacy.

Copyright © 2025 by Raúl Rodriguez

All rights reserved. No part of this book may be reproduced or used in any manner without written permission from the author or publisher except for the use of quotations in a book review or as permitted by U.S. copyright law.

First paperback edition April, 2025

Book design by AquaZebra

Library of Congress Control Number: 2025934739

ISBN 978-1-954604-17-9 (paperback)

Published by AquaZebra

AquaZebra™
Book Publishing
35070 Maria Rd
Cathedral City, CA 92234
mark@aquazebra.com

Raúl Rodriguez
rrdzmasterpo@gmail.com

Dedication

To all those who proudly served the United States
and were betrayed by the government.

Table of Contents

Introduction vii
Chapter 1: Macho Men 1
Chapter 2: SHU Program.. 5
Chapter 3: Runnin' Rattler 11
Chapter 4: Potato Head 17
Chapter 5: The Hamburglar 21
Chapter 6: The Slaughterhouse 27
Chapter 7: Sailing Away 33
Chapter 8: K-Mart Cop 37
Chapter 9: The Texas Ranger... 43
Chapter 10: A Life of LimbLimbo 51
Chapter 11: Transition to Hell 57
Chapter 12: Everyday Temptations..................................... 63
Chapter 13: The Good, the Bad and the Nasty 69
Chapter 14: Okies on the Horizon....................................... 75
Chapter 15: Strapped.. 79
Chapter 16: Praying for Patience 83
Chapter 17: Hittin' the Crossroads...................................... 89
Chapter 18: Shifting Gears 93
Chapter 19: The Application..99
Chapter 20: The Walk of Shame 105
Chapter 21: A Day of Reckoning 111
Chapter 22: Unknown Status 117
Chapter 23: Coconuts and Brownies.................................121
Chapter 24: The Sit Down with CNN................................ 127
Chapter 25: A Man with No Country 131
Epilogue 137

Never look down on anyone unless you're picking them up.
You never know what one is going through.

—Anonymous

Introduction

My name is Raul Rodriguez. Until 2018, I believed I was a U.S. citizen. I served in the United States Navy from June 1992 till September 1997. I worked for Customs and Border Protection from November 2000 to June 2019.

On April 18, 2018, I was asked by my superiors to turn in my gun and badge. Then came the crushing blow. I was informed I was not a U.S. citizen. I almost fell face-first on the floor. I couldn't believe it. At first, I thought it might be a joke. The look on my superiors' faces killed that thought instantly. They weren't smiling.

That being said, I was officially employed with CBP till June of 2019. This went against all policies and protocols for a government position, especially for a federal officer. In the aftermath, I was told I had three years to gain citizenship. This would allow me to get my job back.

In my mind, I was climbing Mount Everest with no oxygen tanks. I would be unable to ever work for CBP again. I wasn't fooled nor did I suffer from delusions of grandeur. My superiors made this clear when I was advised to not speak of my situation. They told me if I did, my chances of getting deported would go up tenfold.

Until February 2020, the U.S. government tried to sweep my story under the rug. The almighty secret they didn't want people to hear. They refused to acknowledge my situation or

A Government Secret

move my case forward. Why? Simply put, they knew it would have a negative reflection on them.

How could an undocumented immigrant be guarding U.S. borders for almost twenty years? Ask them. They set the guidelines, hiring processes, background checks, and so forth. I never broke the law in any shape or form.

This is my unvarnished, true story of how the U.S government has treated an undocumented, disabled veteran—one who diligently fought and worked for their beloved country, the United States of America.

Never Every day brings new choices.

—Martha Beck

Chapter 1

Macho Men

My life started in a small, secluded ranch town outside Matamoros, Tamaulipas, Mexico. I was born on January 14, 1969. We lived about twenty-five minutes by car to the United States. The city of Brownsville, Texas, was to our north. To our family, the U.S. might as well have been Dubai. We loved our home, and I never dreamt of going to the U.S. Ever. It just didn't seem to be in my cards. I would later learn otherwise.

My parents were Margarito and Francisca Rodriguez. I had seven siblings (four sisters and three brothers)—a total of eight kids. Counting my parents, ten people were in my family—pretty standard for most Mexican families. No matter the financial status, you'll rarely see a small Mexican family. It just doesn't exist.

Another thing you'll rarely see in Mexico is men showing any kind of emotion. It's considered a weakness if you do. Men are expected to have hearts of granite; solid and without any cracks or breaks. If someone passes away in the family, you'll see no tears from the men. If someone steals the family car, no emotion from the men. Kids whining for hours, nothing.

I always tried to be the tough kid. We all did to some degree. Life in Mexico was like living in Disneyland—minus the rides. We lived in a farming town that produced nothing but corn and sorghum. At the corner of town, we'd go scavenging for dead bodies. Yes, *dead* bodies. They were dumped in a landfill for dead cartel members.

It was a brutal way of life sometimes. When times are tough, people take chances. Little do they know the risk is *never* worth the reward. If they finally realize that fact, nine out of ten of them are too late.

Farming was the major *legal* form of work. The major *illegal* ways of work were "dope running" and working as "coyotes."

Let me explain further. Dope runners were people who crossed the Rio Grande River with bales of marijuana illegally. I had a friend named Jorge Cervantes who did that for a while. He was a cool dude. Coyotes were young men who would get paid to illegally cross Mexican nationals into the U.S. via the Rio Grande River. It was like Coyote Haven in our little ranch town.

My favorite person on earth was my older sister Amalia. We were super tight and played all day long. She was my ray of sunshine. If she was around, rarely did I have a cloudy day.

My parents would always scold me for being such a *travieso*. Spanish for "mischievous kid." The way they'd get me in line was to say, "Keep acting up and we'll send you to the U.S."

Once I heard that line, I'd go dead silent. I never wanted to go anywhere, let alone the U.S. My biggest fear was being separated from Amalia. I couldn't imagine life without her by my side. The levels of comfort, fun, and happiness she brought me were inexplicable.

It was 1975, and I was having the time of my life. That was, until my parents called me into the kitchen one day. My Dad spoke while my mother remained silent and stone-faced. "Son, we're sending you to live with your aunt and uncle in the U.S. You'll get a great education, and plus, you were born in the United States."

I almost shit myself on the kitchen floor. I never knew I was a U.S. citizen. Mexico was my home, the place I wanted to be forever. To hell with the U.S.! I cried until my brain and eyeballs were dry. It didn't matter. Their minds were made up. When you're a kid, you have no say. You do as you're told. Plain and simple.

My mind went racing as I gazed north towards the U.S. *How the hell did this happen?* I thought. I tried thinking of ways to escape and or stay. Nothing came to fruition, nor did it matter. I'd be leaving Amalia, my family, and my life in Mexico.

The day came when I packed my bag and headed out the door. I hugged Amalia and said bye to my other siblings. I didn't want to go. Something told me I was headed towards Satan's den. Just a gut feeling.

Note to self: Always trust your gut.

When the prison doors are opened,
the real dragon will fly out.

—Ho Chi Minh

Chapter 2

SHU Program

I arrived in the U.S. via Progreso, Texas. My aunt and uncle met me there. We'll call them Arturo and Juana. Along with them were my six cousins. Two of them were twins, Junior and Julian. They all greeted me, and my uncle Arturo took my bag. We packed into their Ford van and headed to my new home, a small town in Texas called Mission. I'd soon call it Hell.

I went from an ultimate high to hitting below rock bottom. All in a matter of one day. Once I landed at my new place, verbal abuse started immediately. Arturo and Juana were disciples of the devil in a nutshell. I'll tell you what I mean by that.

My cousins there had practically no rules. They could do no wrong. They were allowed to go get cookies or drinks at night, no questions asked. Go to the neighbors after dark, the same. With me, it was like prison. Once I'd eaten, the kitchen was closed to me, and my lights had to be out by 8:00 p.m. Everyone else could do as they pleased.

When it came to me, I had a "modified" SHU (Special Housing Unit). It's a place where the worst of the worst criminals are placed in U.S. prisons. It's prison *beyond* prison. Twenty-three hours locked down and one hour for recreation. That's exactly how I felt in Arturo and Juana's house. The only thing missing was the steel bars.

The thing that most people don't understand is verbal abuse and its intensity. They didn't need steel bars to keep me locked inside. Their constant belittling and bashing kept me in mental constraints. If you asked me, "Why didn't you run away, idiot?" I was handcuffed by their words. Even if I'd had a running vehicle awaiting, I would've stayed put. The fear of what they might do to me had me frozen like a statue. It was that bad.

To make matters worse, the twins were bastards. I'd be walking through the hall and Junior would be kicking me in the ass—and hard. Julian would pass me by in the living room and sock me in the mouth. I had nobody to turn to; no Amalia, no mother, *nobody*. I'd think to myself, *I have twelve more years of this shit. I'm never going to make it like this.* I was trapped. I fell into a deep depression quickly.

Sitting at the dinner table was always torture. While everyone ate in peace and conversed with each other, nobody acknowledged me. Nobody talked to me or included me in their conversation. The only thing I got was kicks under the table. When Junior and Julian would get up from the table, they'd slap me on the head and say, "Hurry up and finish, idiot." I dreamt of killing them both each night. No six-year-old should ever have those feelings running through their mind. *Ever.*

As I struggled to figure out a way out of this hell, summer was approaching. Arturo came barging in my room one morning and said, "Pack your shit. You're going home for the summer." Once June came around, I saw the light at the end of the tunnel. I'd be going back home for three months. I couldn't wait. Once we got to the town of Reynosa, I'd cross into Mexico by myself. I had my U.S. birth certificate in hand. Legit. I remember Arturo and Juana saying, "Have a good trip, Raul. We can't wait to see you in September."

Yeah, fuck off, I thought. I didn't even look back. One thing Arturo and Juana were *great* at was fooling people. Keeping up a perfect family image. That's all they ever cared about—their image. Other people had no idea how ruthless they were and how awfully they treated me. Their kids were just as bad, especially Junior and Julian. I used to freeze in shock when I'd hear people in Mission tell me, "Your Aunt and Uncle are such wonderful people." *Are you fucking kidding me?* That shit would make my blood boil. *Come visit me sometime and you'll see what they're really like*. As I said: Masters of Foolery.

Once I was back in Mexico, Mission and all about it was erased from my mind. It was like I went through a morality car wash and cleaned all the shit from Mission off of me in one fell swoop. *Fuck that place and those people who called me "family."* I went from physical and verbal abuse daily to the utmost in hugs and love. My parents would ask how it was in U.S. "Fine" was always my answer, and then I'd quickly change the conversation.

I didn't want to hear about them or think of the life I was simply existing through in Mission. That's right, *existing*. I had no life in Mission. I was not living at all. Just existing, like a vegetative state in a wheelchair for life. Alive physically but mentally brain-dead!

Every Summer morning was bright and hot. We'd play as carefree kids from sunrise to sundown. My mother would make the best dinners, and we'd all talk. Every single one of us. I had missed that so much—being part of a family, my family.

Then the end of August came. I knew that in a few days I'd be returning to Arturo and Juana's house. The day came when we went to Progreso to cross back into the U.S. Tears of sadness littered my face as I said goodbye to Amalia, my siblings, and parents. Once across the border, the shitshow started.

Arturo took my bag and said, "We missed you, Raul. Welcome back."

Once I reached the van, Junior socked me in the stomach and said, "Hurry up and get in the van, stupid." Back to the SHU program. My only thought was that I had to survive nine months till the next summer. It seemed like nine hundred years away in my mind. I had to keep my head on straight. I knew I was on my own.

I fell deeper and deeper into depression. As the years went by slowly, I sank. Summers were my only form of hope, of light. I used to climb a high tree in the backyard and hope I'd die. I didn't want to eat or drink anything. I didn't care to live. I would get cold chills throughout my body because I was so empty inside. The loneliness eroded my life the way acid does metal.

My thoughts of suicide became a morning thought. It felt like I didn't even have organs in my body. My life was described best as walking dead. I'd wake up in the morning and say, "Fuck." I was pissed off because I woke up. Every morning, that four-letter word came out. That or being awoken by the twins with a cold glass of water to the face. Either way, I hated every morning there. Those who never experienced abuse will never understand how those invisible scars affect you. They are far more damaging than physical scars.

That was just the beginning. School life was another ball of wax. My fight continued in and out of the house. I was a prisoner, and my parole date was set for June 1987.

If it doesn't challenge you, it doesn't change you.

—Fred DeVito

Chapter 3

Runnin' Rattler

I only attended one school my entire life: Sharyland School, located at 1216 N. Shary Road. It was a small town, so Sharyland was kindergarten through twelfth grade. Our school mascot was the Rattler, as in rattlesnake. Our school colors were red and white.

One thing I improved at throughout the years was fighting. Most of the kids at school were *guavas*, Spanish slang for *guavachos* or "white boys." I used to get called derogatory words like "wetback" daily. That's all it took, and the punches started. Some I won and some I lost. Through the years, all that shit stopped. I think they saw I couldn't be broken down and eventually fighting ended. But the name calling didn't.

Life went on at Arturo's and Juana's the same as it had begun. I looked forward to summer and that was it. I became known as "the twins' cousin." No name, just that label. I was like their shadow. It fucking irritated me being called that. I never talked, never smiled, and never asked anyone anything. I was in fear of being interrogated by Arturo and Juana. That was their specialty.

One thing they looked forward to doing was interrogating me. It was always "Someone told us you did this at school" or "Someone told us you stole this." Complete bullshit. All mind games. When I would call their bluff and say, "Bring that person here so I can confront them," they'd go quiet. That's when I knew I was onto their games.

I mastered how to walk through their mental minefield. One thing I couldn't beat, though, was the "ghost." The unknown "someone" who was making all the accusations. I didn't fall for that shit. I was becoming mentally stronger as I could see their predictable approaches. It was petty, to be honest.

As I grew older, I'd start crossing the border at Reynosa solo. Birth certificate in my pocket, I'd always get smirks and cold stares from border patrol agents. One day while coming back from Mexico, when I was around thirteen years old, I saw a white border patrol agent. He kept staring me down as I waited in line to enter the U.S. He continued staring, and once I came close to the entrance, he shouted, "Hey you!" I didn't respond. He yelled at me again.

I turned to him and said, "My name isn't 'hey you.'"

I walked to the agent who was checking ID's. Mr. Hey You came up to the agent's desk and said, "Check him out. I think he's illegal."

I laughed and waved my birth certificate in his face. "United States Citizen, bud."

Mr. Hey You snatched the birth certificate out of my hand and started typing at the agent's desk. After ten minutes of haggling, he had a pissed off look on his face. "You can pass through now."

I couldn't hold it in and had to spike the ball. I replied, "Yeah, I know I can." I snatched my birth certificate out of his hand even harder. Once I passed through the gate to enter the U.S. I turned around. He was still staring me down. I gave him the finger and laughed till I cried. I could see that white guy turn as red as a cherry. He couldn't do *shit* to me.

Years went on with the same routine. I was cockier every time I encountered an asshole like Mr. Hey You. It was such a great feeling knowing they couldn't fuck with me. On one crossing, I saw Mr. Hey You and I shouted across the line, "You wanna see my paperwork?" He just look defeated and immediately turned away. I loved sticking it to that prick.

Once I reached my high school years, I saw the light glowing more and more. I only had three years more to go with this abuse and I'd be gone with the wind. I was now fifteen years old.

One day I came home from school and Julian hit me hard on the head. Out of nowhere, no reason. I asked him, "What's your problem?"

He replied, "You're my problem."

I said to myself, *I'm going to kill this motherfucker tonight. In front of Junior, to show him he's next.*

I waited the next night for the twins to come to the room to go to bed. I was prepared. I'd bought a fresh nine-inch Rambo-type knife from the local sporting goods store. My plan was to catch Julian in the room and do his ass right in front of Junior. If Junior tried to be a hero, I'd do him too. I was done with these motherfuckers' abuse. I'd fucking snapped.

Junior came into the room first and jumped on his bed. He didn't acknowledge me. I knew Julian would be close. I couldn't wait to see the look on his face when I started poking holes in his flesh. Once Julian entered the room, I got the drop on him fast. He was dumbfounded. The next thing he saw was my knife pressed hard against his neck. I saw the "bitch" in his eyes. He was scared and he must've seen the devil himself. I was ready to kill this motherfucker.

I wasn't scared. I'd had it. Enough was enough! I wasn't scared of prison or jail. Hell, I was *in* prison here; it was Satan's den. So that shit didn't scare me. I told Julian, "If you or Junior ever lay another hand on me, I'll kill you both. Do you fucking hear me, motherfucker? That goes for you too, Junior. *Am I clear?!*"

All I heard was two little scared whimpers saying, "Yes." I laughed and told them they both might die either way. I slapped Julian across the mouth before pulling the knife back. He held his face like a little girl with tears swelling up in his eyeballs. "Go cry to your fucking parents and see what happens next," I said.

The next day I knew they'd ratted me out when I saw my bed sheets were not the way I'd left them once I returned home from school. Juana must've torn the room apart looking for my blade. You think I would be that stupid to leave it there? Nah. That blade went everywhere with me.

Suddenly, all accusations and physical abuse stopped. Although the verbal abuse from all of them continued, I knew I'd called their bluff, and they folded. They knew it too. If the twins were that tough, they would've tested me. They never tested me or fucked with me again.

Checkmate.

———

My high school years were okay. I found that joining track and choir kept me out of Arturo and Juana's sight even longer. I loved track and ran the 100 meter. It was awesome and I loved competing. I did that for almost two years until I dropped out of it. Choir was more fulfilling for me. Something about music kept me enlightened. I once heard a quote that says, "Music is what feelings sound like." That quote is so true.

The choir competed in the U.I.L. (the University Interscholastic League). We'd compete with schools statewide and nationwide. I loved it. Besides being away from the house of hell, I really enjoyed it. Some of the groups sang in different languages such as German and Italian. It was a wonderful experience.

My prison sentence at Arturo and Juana's finally came to an end. I couldn't believe I'd made it. My graduation was in June 1987. I was cockier and just didn't give a fuck more than ever. Every one of my cousins steered clear of me, including the twins. I was finally going to experience one thing I'd been itching for since 1975: Freedom.

Once graduation came, I packed a bag and went to school. I couldn't wait. My "parole date" was here. I was so ecstatic I couldn't contain myself. Graduation went on for two hours without a hitch. I turned in my cap and gown to the school chancellor and bolted out of his office.

When it was over, I took my parents back to Mexico and never looked back. As I hit the highway, I flipped the bird. I knew I'd never stay another night in that shithole ever. I never said goodbye to Arturo, Juana, or my cousins. That was the end of hell.

After I spent a weekend in Mexico, I crossed back into the U.S. I had a plan in place. My sister Amalia and brother-in-law Martin had a job and place to stay for me in Muleshoe, Texas, six hundred miles away. I couldn't wait to hit the road and see the world. The world I had never known.

I never dreamed about success. I worked for it.

—Estee Lauder

Chapter 4

Potato Head

I hit the road and started my six-hundred-mile trek to Muleshoe. I'd never been there since it was in the northwestern area of Texas. I didn't care. My mind was racing a hundred miles an hour. I felt like Morgan Freeman's character in *The Shawshank Redemption* when he's finally riding the bus, the part where he sticks his head out of the Trailways bus window. Hair blowing in the wind, tasting freedom with each passing mile. That is exactly how I felt. Just passing through plains and fields of agriculture. The air was different. I was free.

Ten hours later I finally reached Muleshoe. I couldn't wait to see Amalia. She had married a nice gentleman named Martin. They had offered me a place to stay and a job, an offer I couldn't refuse. I pulled up to the house and immediately was hugged by Amalia. Martin embraced me after. I settled in and then we sat down to eat some tacos.

Martin and Amalia told me they worked at a potato factory nearby. They had secured me a job there, and I would start on Monday, which was two days away. That gave me time to get a few pairs of jeans, shirts, and hygiene products. Once Sunday night rolled around, Amalia told me, "Raul, we wake up at 3:30 a.m. sharp. Be ready." I was fine with that.

I discovered that 3:30 a.m. came faster than I'd expected, and it was time for work. Amalia set us out three coffees and breakfast burritos. She mentioned to me, "Make sure you always eat breakfast before you go to work." I soon understood what she meant.

We reached the potato factory around 4:45 a.m. This place was huge. Tons of equipment, trucks, and trailers littered the yard. The warehouse was just as big. Many workers were waiting outside for the door to open. Around 4:55 a.m., the foreman (we'll call him "Ben") opened the door. He was one of the few white guys on the site. Once the door opened, people lined up to get their assignments. I waited for my name to be called. I'd lost Amalia and Martin in the sea of workers. Eventually, I heard, "Rodriguez, Raul!"

I replied, "Here."

All I heard Ben say was, "Packing line, row two."

A worker pointed me to the packing line, and I found row number two. I could see ten rows.

At 5:00 a.m. on the dot, a bell rang. It was time to start work. No coffee before or chit-chat with workers. Once that bell rang, work commenced immediately.

My job was to stack one-hundred-pound sacks of potatoes on a pallet. Once I did, a picker would take the sack to the shrink wrapper and load it onto an awaiting trailer. It was some of the hardest work I'd ever done. Heavy lifting all day long. We only got one thirty-minute break for lunch and that was it. The hours were 5:00 a.m. – 5:00 p.m., Monday through Friday. They paid me minimum wage. I didn't care; it beat being at Arturo and Juana's prison.

Plus, I was saving all my money this summer so I could go to college. My plans were to enroll in a technical school of some sorts. I had chosen DeVry Institute in Irving, right outside of Dallas. I was thrilled and worked hard anticipating this next step.

Computers and electronics always got me excited. I always liked to break down computers, toys, you name it. I loved finding the solutions.

———

The end of August came, and it was my last day at the potato factory. I cashed my last check and packed up my bag. I had a one-way Greyhound ticket to Irving. It was about four hundred miles east of Muleshoe, an eight-hour bus ride.

Martin and Amalia dropped me off at the bus station. We hugged and I thanked them both for all their help. They had thrown me a lifeline when I had no other option. Now I was going to DeVry Institute in Irving with money to survive. Amalia always came through no matter what.

At 7:00 a.m., my bus loaded up and I was on my way to Irving. They said we'd get to Irving around 4:30 p.m. with all the stops. I didn't care; I was seeing things I'd never even fathomed. I was on my way. The anticipation was burning inside my heart. I was finally *living*.

Bite into a burger and taste pure bliss.

—Unknown

Chapter 5

The Hamburglar

Riding on the Greyhound bus to Irving was quite a trip. I had so many thoughts blazing in my head I couldn't think. On one of our first stops, a tall Black guy sat next to me (we'll call him Darren). He was very nice, and he asked me where I was going. I told him I was going to be attending school in Irving. I enjoyed talking with him. To be honest, he was the first Black guy I'd ever seen.

In Mission, the population was all white Mexican. Nothing else. I felt happy I was already meeting new people. Towards the end of the trip, he asked me if I had a ride. I told him no, and Darren offered to give me a ride once he met his brother at the bus station.

We arrived in Irving around 5:00 p.m. Darren's brother was waiting, and they embraced. He let his brother know they'd be giving me a ride. His brother said, "Hop in!"

We first stopped at their apartment. Darren offered me the chance to shower, which I accepted. Once I was freshly cleaned, he told me I could leave my bag there. We took off and they dropped me off at my "dorm" in Irving. I thanked them both and went to check in to my new place. One thing missing: my bag.

I met some friends there and checked into my new two-bedroom, one bath apartment. It was like a dorm for DeVry students. Two students assigned to each room. I told a few buddies I left my bag at Darren's but forgot where that was. I hadn't been anywhere, let alone a big city. After a week or so, we finally found Darren's and got my bag back. I was happy to have my clothes.

School life was exciting. I was enrolled in their engineering/electronics program. During the first month, a lot of students dropped out. The hours were 7:00 a.m.–1:00 p.m. I spent my time napping after classes. I'd study at the library until it was time to go to work. I had gotten a job at the local Jack in the Box fast-food restaurant. Minimum wage, but the job had its perks.

It was a five-mile walk to work. I was beginning to run on "empty." I'd get maybe four hours of sleep per day if I was lucky. Sometimes in class I'd be dozing off. My buddy Jake would bump my seat to wake me up. "Raul, you're snoring," he'd whisper. *"Wake up!"* Things like this were normal. I was wearing out. Another problem was my diet: nothing but coffee, cigarettes, and burgers from work.

I worked with a guy named Chino. Our manager, Miguel, was a cool guy. Chino and I would cook a lot of burgers, fries, onion rings—you name it. Usually towards the end of the shift. We were supposed to throw all cooked items away at the end of shift. Instead, Chino and I would take all that food home. Miguel knew what we were doing, but he didn't care. Thinking back, Jack in the Box kept me fed. I never went hungry.

One thing I started to notice was that, when I got home, a lot of the DeVry students would be waiting for me. "Raul, did you bring any burgers?" I'd be feeding half the dorm. Soon, I'd be bringing home big bags of food. We were all struggling, and I was Robin Hood of the dorm. Students would always be waiting even when I arrived late.

After a few days of this, I felt a nasty pain in my stomach. I couldn't move, had no appetite, and I was sweating profusely. This went on for a few days until my friend Gabriel told me I needed to go to the hospital. He offered to take me, and off we went.

Once I was admitted, I saw the nurse come into the room. She had my test results and looked worried. "We need to take you into surgery immediately. Your appendix has burst."

Next thing you know, we're hauling ass to surgery. I remember nothing after that. I woke up the next day and was surprised. All I heard was the cries of thousand babies—newborns.

I don't know how the hell or why I was put there, but I was. I was in the section where newborn babies stayed. The constant crying and whining made my head hurt. I couldn't sleep, let alone have a moment of peace. The situation sucked.

After six days I was discharged. I started towards the door and froze in my tracks. It was *snowing*. I had never seen snow fall before. All I had was a T-shirt and jeans. What the hell was I going to do now?

I had a sheer moment of anxiety to the point of panic. *I am so fucked!* I thought. I kept staring out the hospital window watching the snow fall. I had no ride, no money, no jacket. If I went to walk home, I'd freeze to death. Bear in mind, this was a time before cell phones. I felt sicker than I did pre-surgery. I was *doomed*. I began choking in panic.

In an act of desperation, I called the one phone number I had. It was to Arturo and Juana's. I made a collect call and surprisingly it was accepted. It was Juana who received my call. She was happy to hear from me and asked how I was. My first thought was, *She must have her friends over.* Always an act. At that point, I let her know I was in the hospital and my appendix had burst. Just wanted her to let my parents know since they didn't have a phone in Matamoros. She said, "Yeah, we'll let them know. Hope all is well. Gotta go now. Take care. Bye." *Click*. I knew she didn't give a shit, but hey, I was desperate.

Suddenly, a ray of sunshine lit up my day. My work friend Marcos had just walked into the hospital. I called his name, and we hugged each other tight. "Where have you been Raul? Someone told me you got sick." I told Marcos my appendix had burst, and I had just been released. He asked me what I was going to do; he said he was going to the "valley." That's what people in Mission called the area, referring to the Rio Grande Valley. He asked if I wanted to go with him.

"Hell, yeah!" I replied.

We were on the road heading towards Mission. School, my job—all of it went out the window. I needed a break.

It doesn't matter how much milk you spill
as long as you don't lose the cow.

—Unknown

Chapter 6

The Slaughterhouse

After my mini vacation, we headed back to Irving. I went back to DeVry, ready to catch up on my classes. Once in class, I was summoned to meet the dean in his office. I knew it wasn't good news. The dean told me I was too far behind to catch up in my classes. In DeVry, it was a constant learning session with all cylinders firing. I had missed a whole week. He told me I'd have to drop out and hopefully restart next semester. I knew that wasn't in my cards.

For me to wait around was not a real option. I had a minimum-wage paying job at Jack in the Box and now I was no longer a student. On top of that, I'd gotten my girlfriend, Gloria, pregnant. She'd be giving birth in two months and lived in Matamoros. A good friend of mine, Javier, told me there was a lot of work to be found in Corpus Christi. Once Gloria moved to Texas with me, we got married and had our daughter, Daira.

Now shit got crucial. Now I had a wife and baby girl. I needed to haul ass and get a career jump fast. It was Corpus or bust.

———

Javier, Gloria, Daira and I headed 160 miles north to Corpus Christi. I got a job at a local slaughterhouse. Of all places; I couldn't believe it. Well, I asked for change so there it was. Every imaginable disgusting job you can think of, I did it there.

It was like Shamrock Meats in the movie *Rocky*, but worse. The stench inside was the worst—like a landfill. I'd sweep up cow guts, cut up loins, kill cows, everything. The hardest thing I did was skinning the cows. I got so fast at the job, I'd be able to skin two cows in one minute. Sometimes, the cows would still be alive. They'd be groaning in pain, yet I'd keep on cutting. I lost about twenty pounds working there. It sucked but I had a family to support. I kept thinking in my head, *I've got to find something better than this.*

Javier kept telling me to join the military. He said it was better than being in the meat-processing factory. I went to the Army recruiter and took a test. About a week later, they called me back. I was excited. The recruiter's first words shot my soul out of the sky: "Raul, you suffer from hearing loss. You're a liability and we cannot take you in."

So much for a career in the military. I was bummed. I went back to skinning cows and smelling like a dumpster every day. I felt robotic day after day.

A year passed by with the same routine. I was still trying to look for a better job but to no avail. Money was tight and it always seemed like a miracle to make ends meet each month. When you are barely making it, or falling short of making it, the anxiety you get is gut wrenching. It always came towards the end of each month when most of the bills were due.

About a year later, Javier said I should try the military again. He was always motivating me and looking out for my best interests. Just to shut him up, I went to the U.S. Navy Recruiting Center in downtown Corpus. I was bent on showing Javier this was a waste of time. The Army had already denied me.

I went along anyway and stepped into the Navy Recruiting Center. A short, dark-skinned Filipino stood up. He was in his khakis and introduced himself as Petty Officer De La Cruz. I told him my name and explained my situation. I did tell him about my strikeout at the Army a year earlier. He asked me what I was doing these days. I told him, "Pissing my life away slaughtering cows." He chuckled and told me to sit down. He had a big grin on his face.

De La Cruz told me he was retiring in thirty days. He was short and promised me a career in the Navy. I told him about my hearing loss; he told me not to be worried.

The next day, we went to the M.E.P.S. (Military Entrance Processing Station). I was given a battery of hearing tests. After half a day there, De La Cruz drove me home. Before I got out of the vehicle, he said, "Raul, I'll call you once I get those results."

I waved bye and walked inside the house. In my gut, I didn't give this a chance.

The next afternoon, De La Cruz called. He told me my hearing wasn't too bad, and he said he could get me in. He told me I'd have to leave at a moment's notice once a slot opened. I told him, "Okay," and gave it no more thought. I was the "seeing is believing" guy. I went back to the meat-processing plant and continued my life of skinning cows.

About two weeks later, my foreman, Beto, called me to the front office. I washed my hands and walked to find him. Once I got to Beto's office, he pointed to the window. "He's here for you, Raul." There stood De La Cruz in his Navy whites. It was like a scene from the movie *Officer and a Gentlemen* with Richard Gere and Louis Gossett, Jr.

Beto had a big grin on his face and said, "You're done here, Raul. Let's go. No need to get anything. You won't be coming back here." That was music to my ears. The conditions were horrible, and I hated that job. I threw off my coat and hard hat in a second. I waved goodbye to Beto and never looked back.

De La Cruz made it simple as he drove me home. It was around 3:00 p.m. "Raul, you leave for boot camp tomorrow. Get drunk, tell your wife and family goodbye, but be ready at 8:00 a.m. sharp. I did hurdles for you to get in." He had, too. I really appreciated De La Cruz, and he was a man of his word.

The clock was ticking now. I had seventeen hours of freedom left. It was June 1992. I would be heading to Orlando, Florida, for boot camp.

You never know how strong you are,
until being strong is the only choice you have.

—Bob Marley

Chapter 7

Sailing Away

I was on my way to the airport the next morning. I was excited about being in the military and what the Navy was going to be like. I was excited to be an aircraft mechanic and find a career after the military doing that. I was already pre-planning to get a job at a place like Raytheon, Boeing, or McDonnell-Douglas. Little did I know that wasn't the way it was going to play out.

Recruiters for the Armed Forces always promise you the world. They'll tell you it's easy to switch jobs while you're in. That's total bullshit. If it's not on your contract, you're not getting it. Plain and simple. They lie to each of our gullible asses just to get us in. For me, it really didn't matter. I needed a change from working a dead-end job. Plus, I wanted to improve my family's quality of life. Sometimes you need to sacrifice to get ahead. It's the only way.

Once in Orlando, we were shipped in buses to the base for a nine-week boot camp. It was humid as hell, and it seemed to rain everyday there. I was part of the first integrated class which would include both males and females. The time there went fast, and after nine weeks, I was done and off to my first permanent duty station. I got my orders: I was being sent to Jacksonville, Florida.

Being a part of the Navy was okay for me. I enjoyed the traveling and the daily routines. The one thing that sucked was

A Government Secret

being away from my family. It was not like today's military, where you have many opportunities to visit your loved ones. We often deployed on six-month tours, floating around the globe. I held many jobs there, including being a cook. My favorite assignment was when I became an MA (Master at Arms). It's the Navy's military police.

Except for times when I was stationed in places like Jacksonville, San Diego, and a few others, I was always afloat on a ship. I sailed on the USS New Orleans, which also carried marines aboard.

Ship life sucked, to be honest. Lots of playing cards, listening to music, working out and training. It was a "twelve on, twelve off" work schedule. We slept in three-high cots that were super tight. We called them "coffins." (I heard that, on submarines, the bunks were four-high. I guess we had no right to complain.)

Military life made me super fit. Being five feet, five inches and 140 pounds, I was in the best shape of my entire life.

The biggest perk of being afloat on a ship was the countries we'd visit. During my time in the Navy, I visited so many exotic places. Of course, some were not so exotic.

Some of the places I got to visit were Australia, Bahrain, the Persian Gulf, Jordan, Hong Kong, Singapore, UAE, Japan and Hawaii. I'm sure I'm forgetting a few, but it was great to see different cultures. I'd be the guy that would try the different foods they had to offer. Some were great and some garbage. The entire journey was an incredible experience.

Around October 1994, while on the USS New Orleans, I met a guy named Ronald. He was a cool, white guy who always was reading the pamphlets. I got nosy and asked him what he was reading. He told me he was looking for a career after the military. We each had around a year and a half left, so he was thinking about the future.

I, on the other hand, lived day by day. Ronald often told me, "Raul, you should join me. I'm going to be applying for the INS [the Immigration and Naturalization Service]." He told me the pay was good, and the benefits for families were top notch. I told him I'd think about it. One thing Ronald said to me stuck with me: "If you don't think about a career, you'll be working minimum wage jobs till you die."

I thought of the slaughterhouses and immediately shit bricks. I replied to Ronald, "The INS, huh?"

We hang the petty thieves and
appoint the great ones to public office.

—Aesop

Chapter 8

K-Mart Cop

Once I left the military in the fall of 1997, I needed to get my ass in gear. I was divorced, had two kids, and wanted a career that could give my kids all the amenities they needed. I really had been thinking about a career with the INS. The reason this was very personal to me was, I wanted to make a change. Even if it was small, I wanted to make changes in the system. I'd been hassled my whole life crossing back and forth into Mexico.

Border agents always questioned my U.S. status, but my paperwork was ironclad. I vowed not to ever be a prick like the many agents I encountered as a kid. My packet had been sent in and I always kept up on updates and status checks. Back then, it was all by telephone; cell phones weren't available yet. I waited patiently, but I still had bills and a family to raise. In the meantime, I got a security job working at different posts.

Some of these security posts were boring. Sometimes I'd be sent to meaningless posts. One I can remember was a construction site to guard materials, making sure nobody came through in the night and robbed the site of the goods. I thought it was funny since I never thought that would occur much.

Occasionally on my rounds, I'd see a truck pull up near the main gate. You could tell they were looking for a breach. I'd shine my flashlight on them, and they'd take off immediately. Some of these bandits would cruise the town looking for an unguarded site. Nobody was going to breach my post. I took my job seriously.

Another assignment was guarding a car dealership, a boring-ass gig. The gate stayed closed so it was nearly impossible to break through the steel structure. I felt secure in the lot. Occasionally I'd doze off for a thirty-minute catnap. The biggest excitement I got during this post was hearing stray cats fighting and jumping from car to car. Some job, huh? I longed for something with action; preferably a day job, if possible. This graveyard shift was a pain.

Sleep was a thing of the past. Being on graveyard shift, I'd usually get four hours of sleep out of 24—if I was lucky. Having two kids doesn't permit you much rest. I'd sleep all I could while they went to school.

I called my boss, Armando, who ran our posts. I told him I needed a day/swing shift. I didn't care what or where. I needed to get on a normal shift. He told me he'd switch me in a week. After ten days, I thought he'd blown me off. *What an asshole,* I thought.

A few days later, I got a call from Armando. He told me he had not forgotten about me. The call was music to my ears. "Raul, I got you a post at the local K-Mart. The hours are 10:00 a.m.–7:00 p.m. Lots of action, and you won't be bored, I assure you that. You interested?"

"Hell, yeah, I'm interested! When do I start?" I asked him.

He told me, "Friday, so be prepared."

I was so excited.

K-Mart was the Walmart of the '70s, '80s and '90s. It was a huge department store chain that had many stores across the U.S. The store sold everything you could think of: major appliances, tools, guns, toys, sporting goods—you name it. Plus, they sold food items, like ICEEs, popcorn, and hot dogs. The stores look small compared to Walmarts of today. Back then, though, it was the go-to store.

Armando had told me to report to a guy named Darren. I went to the store at 10:00 a.m. sharp that Friday. As I walked in, I asked for Darren in Loss Prevention. A few minutes later, a big white guy walked up to the counter. He looked annoyed as we locked eyes. He said, "Can I help you? I'm Darren."

I told him I was there to report for security. He shook his head and almost laughed. *"You?"* he sneered. *"A security guard? Really?"*

I told him yes, and he immediately grabbed the phone to make a call. About a minute later, a tall Mexican guy came up to the desk. Darren introduced him as his partner, Danny. They looked up and down at my five-foot-four-inch, 140-pound frame. I heard Darren utter to Danny, "What the fuck did they send us? A seventh grader? What's *he* going to do when we have shoplifters willing to fight?"

Danny shook his head and left the counter without saying anything else. They both had disgust for me right off the gate. Darren told me that when they had shoplifters, car thieves, purse snatchers, I'd have to report to the areas immediately. He went back to the office shaking his head. I knew I'd have to prove myself. I wouldn't have to wait long for that.

———

The next day, I got a radio call from Darren. He told me they had a couple coming out that had stolen items. I stopped them as Darren and Danny made their way out behind them. The guy swung at me, but I ducked and jumped on his back. He fell immediately and Danny slapped the cuffs on him. I also had his legs twisted. The woman was cuffed as well. They had over five hundred dollars of stolen merchandise on them. As

Darren and Danny let them back in the store, I heard them say, "He might work out after all."

Many similar incidents continued over time. I'd see it all, from old ladies stuffing make-up in their undergarments to young guys running out with toolboxes. If I was on shift, they wouldn't get away. Darren and Danny would eventually rave to the store manager about me. A month later, Darren called me into the office via radio. He and Danny were eating lunch. "Pull up a chair. We got you lunch." I knew I'd passed the test.

One particular incident was a guy who was trying to break into a car. I walked up to him and asked what he was doing. I saw a shiny, .357 Magnum revolver glimmering in the man's hand. He spoke softly: "Don't be a hero, youngster. Get back or I'll blast your ass."

Oh, shit. I put my hands up and backed away. "You got it." That was a close call. He took off running afterwards.

The craziest incident at K-Mart had to be one involving a muscle-bound dude stealing tools. This Mexican had to be 275 pounds, solid. He looked like he'd been pumping iron in prison for a decade. Danny called over the radio: "Raul, he's coming out. Stop him. He's a big dude. We're coming."

As soon as this monster came out, he saw me running toward him. He got into a three-point football stance and came at me full force. I pivoted and swung onto his back. He was swinging me around and I could feel my legs crashing into the vending machines outside. I could hear wrenches clinking on the ground as they fell out of the guy's pants. Darren and Danny started tackling his legs, but this guy was super strong. I had him in a chokehold, but we probably looked like a fly on a bear.

After a minute, which seemed like forever, the guy started getting weak. All three of us struggled to get this guy down. I told him, "You can stop now. I'm not letting you go." Just like that, the guy dropped to the floor, exhausted. Darren cuffed the dude with two sets of handcuffs. This dude made Lou Ferrigno look small. As we walked back inside, Darren and Danny said, "Good job, Raul! We love having you here."

Size doesn't matter. It's what you got inside that counts the most.

———

After an extensive investigation three years later, I received a letter from the INS. It was my acceptance letter, saying I was to report in two weeks to the Progreso, Texas, station in business attire. I couldn't believe it. I had thought they'd forgotten about me.

I showed up in jeans and a collared shirt two weeks later. The administrator asked me if I had read clearly that it was "business attire." I told him I didn't own a suit. He told me to report back the next day.

This time I showed up in fresh new slacks, collared shirt and tie, and dress shoes. He told me I would be going to Brunswick, Georgia, for training. The place was called FLETC (the Federal Law Enforcement Training Center). It was the primary training site for all major federal agencies. I was excited. The year was 2000. What a way to start off!

Learning never exhausts the mind.

—Leonardo DaVinci

Chapter 9

The Texas Ranger

Once I got to Georgia, we were bused in from the airport. There were many candidates from different agencies. We all talked on the way to FLETC. It was a co-ed and richly diverse group. Some of the passengers were going for the INS like me. Others were going to agencies like ATF (Alcohol, Tobacco and Firearms), FBI (Federal Bureau of Investigation), CBP (Customs and Border Patrol), to name a few. Once we got to the facility, it was like the first day of bootcamp. Everyone was screaming and yelling at us "recruits." This would be our home for the next three months.

We were assigned to two-resident rooms that resembled the military. During these three months, we'd learn how to shoot, drive at high speeds, practice self-defense, and study INS laws. The school part, which included all the laws, was extensive. So many INS laws pertained to the slightest of issues. I was overwhelmed at first, but I eventually started gliding. I just had to pay attention. I took daily notes and tested myself with other INS candidates.

During this time in the academy, I met a beautiful woman named Anita. She was in my class, and we started hanging out in our off time. I told her about my life and my two kids. She was quite astute, and I was blown away. I was hoping we'd end up at the same duty station upon graduation. Something about her was special; she was unlike any woman I'd ever been with.

Within two weeks of graduation, we were all handed "dream sheets"; that's what they were called in the military. They were basically a sheet with three lines. The students would list three destination spots where they wanted to be placed. Typically, you never get what you wanted—at least, that's what it was like in the military.

I ended up getting the spot I desired, which was at the Progreso, Texas, station. Anita got a spot in San Luis, Arizona, which sucked. I promised to keep in touch with her. I was just happy to not be stationed at Laredo station. Nobody wanted Laredo since it was the busiest of all border crossings, nicknamed the "dope pipeline," due to the traffic of Interstate 35; busts happened there almost daily. I-35 went all the way up to Wisconsin and crossed all other major interstates, cutting straight through the Midwest. I was lucky to have dodged that bullet.

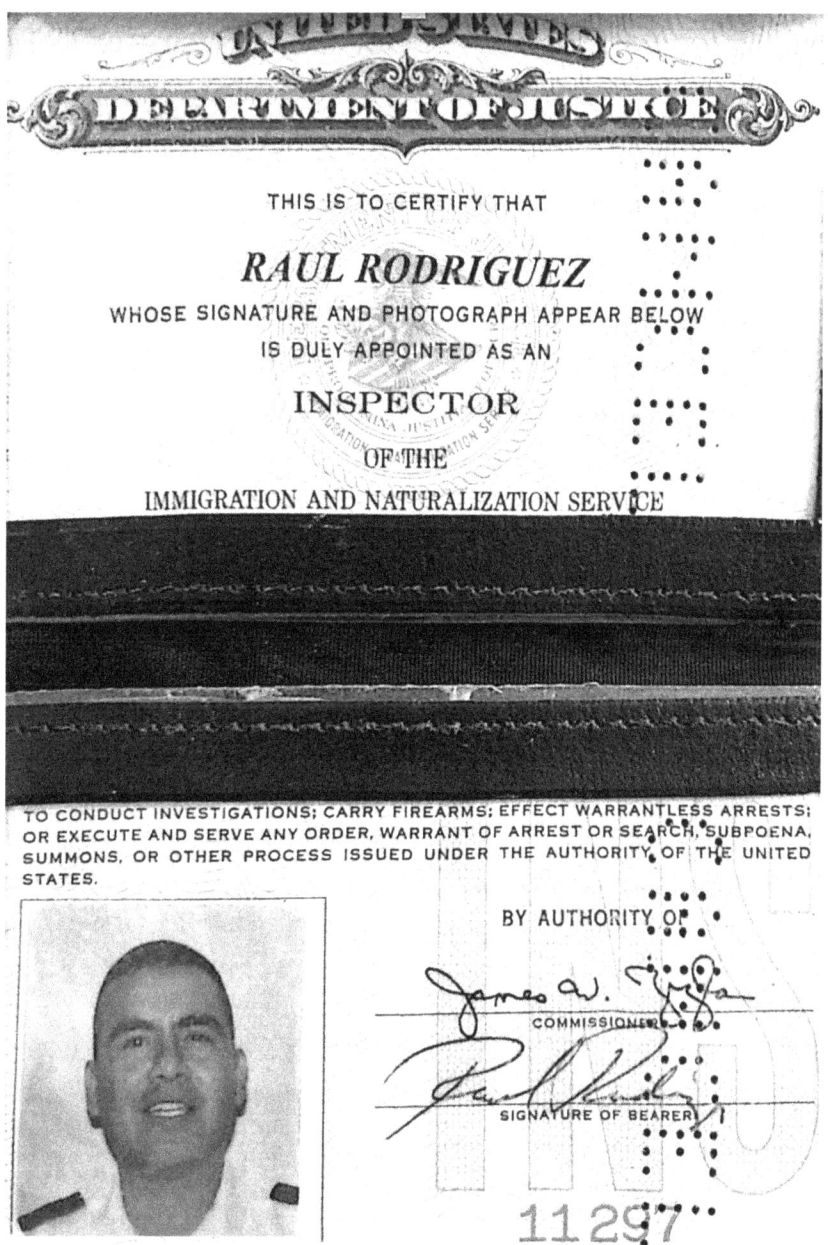

My first day on the job was intense. I didn't know what to expect, but I was ready. I showed up to the Progreso station in my INS uniform (white shirt and black pants). I had my full gun belt attached to my person. My supervisor was called "Mr. T." He was a seasoned agent who knew his shit. I ended up learning a lot of game from Mr. T. He showed me all the ins and outs of the law. Plus, he showed me what to look for on the job.

Mr. T would have me read the INS "bible." All the laws were in one book. He'd test me daily and loved seeing my progress. Every chance I had I studied these laws. I had so many to learn, and I hand-wrote all my notes. (An I-Pad back then would've helped big time.) One thing I used to do a lot of was smoking cigarettes. I'd get called by Mr. T who smoked like a train. When he passed by my station, he'd yell out, "Rodriguez, let's go smoke." I loved it.

At the Progreso station, we worked two bridges: The Progreso and Los Indios crossings. A lot of INS staff were dinosaurs back then; they didn't want to learn new things and believed they knew it all. Mr. T would always tell me, "Don't become complacent like them, Rodriguez. You won't learn shit and you won't move up in the ranks." That stuck with me.

One issue that the INS had was the ever-changing laws. The DOJ (Department of Justice) would amend all the methods for processing illegal immigrants. The problem was, they were written by college grads in Washington, DC, who had never seen a border crossing nor its challenges. This caused a lot of headaches for us.

I began to get serious with Anita, who was still in Yuma, Arizona. We'd see each other whenever we could, but mainly we connected by e-mail and pay phones. I'd make sure I always had a roll of quarters in my car and change in my pocket. By now, it was February 2002, and we had been making big plans. I knew we'd eventually be together and get married. She was my rock, my diamond in the rough. I felt blessed to be with her.

Contraband coming across the border was always a "30-40-30" method. Thirty percent of catches were food and agricultural material. Food can carry certain insects or spoil. Once it spreads, you're screwed. Forty percent of the seized material was drugs and merchandise. Drugs were hidden everywhere. I'd see drugs hidden in quarter panels, near the motors, under the spare tire, and so forth.

The last thirty percent of seized material consisted of people—illegal immigrants. They'd often be caught at the checkpoint. They would always give themselves away by avoiding eye contact. Sometimes we'd find them hiding in trunks.

It was a constant learning experience. I loved it all and treated people like human beings. I wasn't going to be like those pricks I encountered as a kid.

Lots of Americans crossing into Mexico would go for medication. When you'd go to Mexico, you'd find everything you need at any pharmacy. You'd pay a quarter of what you'd pay in the U.S.—if that. A lot of elderly people couldn't pay the price and sought a less expensive way. Still, it was illegal and if caught, they'd lose their medications purchased in Mexico.

The most exciting times came when we had a drug bust. I remember this old man who resembled Clint Eastwood in the movie *The Mule*. He pulled up in a beat-up Dodge truck. He locked eyes with me when he hit my checkpoint. I smelled that something wasn't right. I had him pull into the secondary station. Sure enough, another agent flagged me over.

When you go through a secondary checkpoint, the examination is much more thorough. Cars might go through an Xray machine to spot anomalies. This truck had plenty in the gas tank. We pulled the gas tank off and could see bricks inside. It was loaded with marijuana. The old man's demeanor changed once he saw the bricks of marijuana coming out. He knew he was done.

I felt bad for this guy, but I knew I had a job to do. Seeing an eighty-year-old man in handcuffs never sat well with me. I often wondered what drove someone to roll the dice with their freedom. Mr. T said it best: *money* and *greed*.

The greatest nations are defined
by how they treat their weakest inhabitants.

—Jorge Ramos

Chapter 10

A Life in Limbo

Working for the INS had many curveballs. One of those was, they were terribly short on staff—not just them, but other agencies like ICE as well, not just in Southern Texas but everywhere in the United States. Immigration management was always an enormous effort nationwide. The people that just read the news don't get the full story of the situation on the Southern Border. Most immigrants aren't just Mexicans; many are from other countries. Some journeys have been riskier or farther just to make it to Mexico. When Mexicans get caught crossing the border illegally, they're usually bussed across the border.

Central Americans and South Americans were much of the other half. Central Americans come from places like Guatemala, Panama, Honduras, and El Salvador. South Americans come from places like Peru, Colombia, Argentina, etc.

The Chinese were part of the immigrating population, too—Asians in general, but Chinese were the leading Asian race for illegal immigrants coming from the Far East. Chinese come from across the pond. These races can't be driven to their home countries. They need to be flown out by airplane. Here's how this works out.

Say you've got a lot of Brazilian illegals. The U.S. marshals operate a flight service (like the movie *Con-Air*), but this service is specifically for illegals. It's called "JPATS" (Justice Prisoner & Alien Transportation System). They'll wait till they have enough Brazilian illegals to fill a whole flight. Once that happens, they'll fly out a plane full of Brazilian illegals back to Brazil. Same goes for all other illegals from different countries.

One race is a bit more difficult to transport: the Chinese and other Asians. Most Asians are from across the Pacific. The U.S. Marshals won't make a JPATS flight to Beijing for just a handful of Chinese illegals. They must make it "worth it." Most Chinese/Asian illegals are sent to detention centers in big cities like New York City, Los Angeles, San Francisco or Chicago. That way, when there are enough passengers for a JPATS flight, the U.S. marshals won't be "wasting their time."

Sometimes a few of us would accompany the marshals on these flights. I never flew a JPATS flight to China, only to Central and South American countries. It was usually a quick trip, and they were offloaded like cattle. We'd refuel and be back in the air in an hour.

When any illegal immigrant is caught, they are housed at a detention center created strictly for illegals. They will never land in the county jails or state prisons. The INS started sending out e-mails and calls for help. Mr. T let us know they needed help running a detention center outside San Antonio, 250 miles north of Progreso. Away from home. A four-hour drive, to be exact. He asked if anybody was interested. I raised my hand.

"Good, Rodriguez. You'll leave tomorrow. You'll receive lodging at the Holiday Inn near San Antonio. Plus, you'll get per diems. Good luck." He gave me the address of the detention center and the name of the lieutenant in charge. He told me I'd get the lodging address once I arrived there in San Antonio. I hated to be away from my two kids, but I needed to put my time in.

I gave Anita a call and told her about my new "temporary station." She was happy for me and wished me luck. The next morning, I was on my way to San Antonio. They said it would be around two–three months' duty there. I knew it would fly by fast.

The next day around 1:00 p.m., I arrived at the Detention Center. I was greeted by Lieutenant Mouser. He was a tall, white guy with a deep Southern accent. He told me he was happy to have me there. He gave me my lodging address at the Holiday Inn. He asked me if I wanted to take a tour. I said sure, and we walked all around the facility.

I was shocked to see all these people packed in like sardines. I saw the gymnasium-type dorm with rows and rows of bunk beds. A TV sat at each end of the dorm. I figured the number of detainees in one dorm at any given time to be at least 250–300. *One INS officer per dorm!* That was fucking *mind blowing!* I knew if shit hit the fan, I'd be screwed. We couldn't carry our weapons inside, so that left me with my mace.

Another challenge was, we never walked inside the dorm unless it was to give information to someone—or to retrieve someone for fingerprints, photos, and so forth. We'd walk outside on catwalks or the outside hallways. We'd constantly hear the chattering and screaming in Spanish, "What's my status?" "When am I going to be released?" "Who's in charge of this fucking place?" The list went on and on.

To be honest, I loved working at the detention center. Once my eight hours were done, I'd go have dinner in the hotel lobby. Then I'd rest up and call Anita before bedtime. All I did the entire day was process illegals in and out. I never had stress like working at the gates at Progreso. I always had something to do when I worked the line at the borders. Here, processing and babysitting were pretty much the entire job.

The only time it sucked was when I'd have to go inside the dorm to get one or two illegals to finish processing. Imagine: me, all alone, surrounded by 250 illegals, angry and circling me. They'd be doing the usual cursing, begging, and yelling.

Most wanted to know when they were leaving. I couldn't have told them even if I wanted to. It sucked, but that was beyond my pay grade.

Another thing I loved doing was "transports." When a busload or two of illegals were headed to a JPATS flight, we'd escort them to a hangar at the local airport. This hangar was leased by the U.S. Marshals to conduct JPATS flights when needed. Simple and easy.

One day I was in an unmarked car in the lead spot, escorting two JPATS buses to the airport. A man (whom we believed was an illegal) thought we were following him. The truth was, we were lost and looking for a side gate to the hangar. The man drove a beat-up hippie van. Suddenly, he bolted out of his car and started running—*towards the tarmac!* What was he doing?

We kept driving and swung around the other side of the gates. They were locked! We saw the same guy run out of the bushes and haul ass. He must've thought we were following or chasing him. He did a 180 and started running back towards the original turn. We were laughing till we cried. When our convoy made our way back to the original main street, his van was still in the middle of the street. The poor dude ran for nothing.

The inmates would curse at us daily. Lieutenant Mouser said, "We can't tell them shit, Raul. We signed a form saying that when we got hired. You give out information to anyone, you'll be terminated immediately." He was right about that one. The INS was very strict on this. A lot of people sometimes got "lost" in the system and would be incarcerated for a long time.

Since their contacts usually had no means to get their information from the outside, they'd basically be lost in limbo. Their family and friends had no way of getting that information to them. They could obtain a "FOIA" request. That's the Freedom of Information Act, which would tell them their status. The wait time on one of those was a minimum of one year at best. So good luck with that.

One way you could get your status updated in a week or two was to pay a "processing fee." Usually those were expensive since you could only obtain this through a lawyer—one with hefty price tags on them. To retain a lawyer, you'd need deep pockets. Most illegals would come to this country with fifty bucks (if they were lucky) and a gallon of water. Harsh reality, but those were the facts. How the hell could they retain a lawyer charging $400 an hour on the low end? Unless they had a rich family on the outside, they weren't going nowhere till their case was resolved. Like that old joke says, "What do you call a thousand lawyers at the bottom of the ocean? A good start!" LOL.

You must be the change you wish to see in the world.

—Mahatma Gandhi

Chapter 11

Transition to Hell

By 2003, Anita and I were living together. Our relationship had become even more stable. No more traveling long hours to spend a weekend together. I still worked at my original post and Anita worked at the Brownsville post. On June 22, 2007, we made it official; we were married. It was a great joy to have found my soulmate. Things were at an ultimate high for our family.

Around November 2007, the whole INS department got a rude awakening. Nobody saw this coming. Absolutely nobody.

The Department of Homeland Security (DHS) was created on 11/25/02 due to the 9/11 attacks. Most of us didn't buy that. We saw it was just a way to invade your privacy just like the Patriot Act. INS was dissolved into the CBP (Customs and Border Protection). Most of the CBP personnel had no idea how the INS laws worked. It was very tricky. DHS was to oversee all their sister departments. There was just one problem: DHS didn't know shit about immigration laws.

Let me explain.

When we were working under INS, we had laws and guidelines. We never bent or wiggled those laws. They were etched in stone, and matters flowed much easier. When DHS took over, these college grads out of the academy had *zero* experience. What made it even worse was, they thought they knew more than some of us seasoned veterans. We had a ton of tenured personnel on staff. We knew our shit. We had an edge on these youngsters. We had a ton of OTJ—on the job—training. Nothing supersedes that. You can ask any Law Enforcement Officer about that. They'll tell you the same thing I'm telling you now.

Now, it's up to the Port Director who gets deported, who walks, all depending on their mood. That would never have happened with INS. Zero guidelines were in place now. It was basically every day we all felt like the new guys. The job changed every single day—as did the laws. One day it was this set of guidelines, another day it was another set. This created a mass exodus of seasoned personnel. All of this was bad.

A lot of these seasoned personnel took early retirement, walked off the job completely, or quit outright. This was the most damaging thing to happen to DHS. We'd lost all of our expertise, all of our wisdom. What it was replaced with was college grads or vets who'd just been discharged from the service. We were like a handful of personnel in a huge kindergarten class.

The full transition took a solid year. It was a painful one that lasted lifetimes in my head.

I needed to get involved in other things to keep me busy. Or better yet, to keep me from going insane. Seeing some of these egregious calls being made just made me sick. It was like playing Bingo and seeing who'd be the lucky winner of the day. Soon, I'd get some action—and it came out of the sky.

Around Christmas 2007, I recall busting a Hispanic female, Tina, for bringing in eggshells. This was a definite no-no as it could carry the bird flu. She had one of those snapdragon, foul-mouthed attitudes. She screamed louder than a wounded hyena in the Serengeti. Plus, her three children she crossed with always looked ragged and filthy. I felt bad for them. One time, a new CBP agent asked her, "Why don't you give them a bath?"

She turned around and launched a water bottle over his head that barely missed him. *"Go fuck yourself!"* she screamed.

He never told her anything after that. She was a "frequent crosser," at least once a week. She was a U.S. citizen.

One day I stopped at the gas station after work to get a pack of cigarettes. I had to pick up my son from school. I heard someone whistling as I was getting close to my car. It was Tina. She was walking up behind me. She waved me over. I didn't move, so she came over to my car. She hollered, "Hey, border guy, you wanna make some money?"

I asked her what she meant. She explained if I let her illegally cross some kids over, that her "bosses" would compensate me. She told me she illegally crossed kids over from Mexico frequently. She got them false documents and got paid well. For some strange reason, she trusted me immediately. I knew she was "green" once she did. A smart veteran of that game doesn't ever trust anyone—let alone a border agent. Tina asked me what I'd charge per child. I told her, "Three hundred bucks a piece."

She smiled and said, "Okay, here's my number. Let's do it."

Now think about this for a second. I was the dumb one here. The going rate for a person to cross illegally was around two thousand dollars per person at the time. I knew this. I got a smuggler asking me my price, and I told her three hundred dollars per person. She must've thought I was a fucking idiot. Trust me, I felt like one after the fact.

Whenever you get a tip like this, you must notify the OIG (Office of Inspector General—our internal affairs department in a nutshell.) When I took the story to them, they asked me if I wanted to work on this case undercover. I was excited and jumped on the opportunity immediately.

It's mandatory you report this immediately if something like this falls into your lap. A lot of people in the agency live beyond their means and run into deep debt. A clear way out of it is to take bribes from drug/smuggling organizations. These organizations pay top dollar and don't hesitate to pay when they want something done. Money is not an issue. For some, temptation becomes reality. Once you do one favor for these individuals, you're trapped. It's sad, but it's a reality that still exists today.

Tina and I kept in contact for the next few weeks. She'd tell me everything that was happening and offered me sex, dope—you name it. I respectfully declined all offers. She told me she'd done this countless times. Finally, the day came for her to cross three kids illegally. She was excited, but I think I was even more keyed up than she was.

The plan was for Tina to call me. I'd tell her to go to the lane I was working on. Once she crossed over, I'd take off my ballcap for the bust signal for the rest of our team.

She came up to my booth and we played the "U.S. citizen" role. You could see the kids clearly were scared. Once she passed through, I took off my ballcap.

A bunch of agents blocked her vehicle and dragged her out of the car. The kids were taken away by a few other CBP agents. She looked pissed and I could hear her talking shit to the arresting agents. Man, that woman could scream.

Turned out, the case was bigger than smuggling kids. Over the next few years, plenty of stash houses were located. People working for Tina and her boss included local schoolteachers, mechanics, and others. Tina's boss was eventually arrested as well.

Later, I received the second-highest Integrity Award for this case. I felt awesome knowing I had performed well. Still, the headaches with the whole DHS takeover were a catastrophe. The job never was the same. And this was merely the beginning.

Raúl Rodriguez

Integrity Award

Not Pictured: **Raul Rodriguez**
CBP Officer
Progreso, Texas

In recognition of the highest level of professional integrity and loyalty, embracing the values of CBP when confronted with attempted bribery. In June 2006, Officer Rodriguez participated in an undercover sting operation with investigators from the Office of the Inspector General (OIG), resulting in the arrest and Federal prosecution of one person for bribery and attempted alien smuggling. On May 24, 2006, Officer Rodriguez stopped at a local convenience store after ending his shift at the Port of Progreso. He was approached by a woman who told him that she wanted to bring an undocumented person through the port. Under the direction of the OIG, and after several meetings with the woman, Officer Rodriguez was paid a $300 bribe. After clearing primary, the woman and the undocumented alien were apprehended in post primary and turned over to OIG agents.

VIGILANCE ★ SERVICE ★ INTEGRITY

Every moment of resistance to temptation is a victory.

—Frederick Faber

Chapter 12

Everyday Temptations

Working for the CBP came with a lot of power. With power comes major temptations, not just once or twice a week, but every day. You must remember that you are the last line of defense. You dictate what goes through our borders and what doesn't. Whether that involves the trafficking of products or people, the love of money is the root of all evil.

One thing the CBP has always done with their employees is "debt checks." The administration will run your credit and check your debts frequently. It's part of the job and you must accept these conditions. The reason for this procedure is to check to see who's in major debt. If you have major debt, you're more likely to take a bribe. Mexican criminal organizations have got more money than Fort Knox. If you're making $80k–$120k a year as an agent, you're doing well. If you're living beyond your means, you're who these crooked organizations are looking for—someone in financial ruins.

Imagine you're in the hole $100,000 and need to get out of debt immediately. The reality is, no bank is just going to hand you $100,000 in cash and "hope" you get your shit together. Some agents have turned to these criminal organizations in desperate times like these. They believe, *All I've got to do is let one loaded car go through and that'll take care of it.* But that's never the end. What they've done is sold their soul to the devil himself. They're stuck in a web of misery.

A car loaded with kilos of cocaine can be worth well over three to five million dollars. If you let that car go through and get fifty thousand dollars for it, you're halfway out of debt. One more time and you're debt-free! That's the temptation of it. Once you take a dollar from these organizations, they have you by the balls. If you say, "Hey, guys, I quit," they can always comeback with, "No problem. We'll just call your boss." That's prison time, pensions and benefits lost, and so on.

See what I mean? I recall one time, I got busy and forgot to pay my gas bill, something around $150. My superiors called me into the office one day after shift. I was surprised. "Rodriguez, you know you have an outstanding bill that hasn't been paid. Are you running into financial troubles?"

I was completely befuddled. What the hell were they talking about? I asked my superiors, "What outstanding bill?"

One of my bosses grabbed a piece of paper from his desk. He handed it to me and said, "Here's what we're talking about." It was my unpaid gas bill of $150. I had completely forgotten to mail it in. Seven days past due.

I remembered, and I told them I'd get it taken care of ASAP. Can you believe it? They took this kind of shit seriously.

On a few occasions, I have witnessed this myself up close. People who've worked with me side by side. One minute they're in uniform, the next they're wearing chrome bracelets. Being led to a paddy wagon and off to jail. I made a promise to myself I'd never succumb to such temptations. I never wanted to abandon Anita and our kids. I couldn't imagine seeing my family visit me in a cage behind an inch-thick plexiglass window. This very thought kept me in hard check throughout my career.

I recall a time when I really wanted this new Toyota Tacoma truck with big wheels. I kept telling Anita we needed to save for this. I'd seen a few in town and kept drooling over them in magazines.

One day Sammy, a co-worker, saw me reading a truck magazine in the breakroom. "Rodriguez, you still looking at that truck?" he asked. I told him I was, but it was just too expensive for our budget. Sammy was his typically frugal self and said, "Save up for it." And with that, he left the breakroom.

About four months later, Sammy rolled up to work in a gorgeous red Corvette, the newest model at the time. I was amazed and told him it was a nice car. The week after that, he rolled in to work on a brand new Harley Davidson motorcycle. Something wasn't right. "Mr. Frugal" had become Howard Hughes. Practically overnight. One day after shift, Sammy told me he could get me that Toyota Tacoma truck for half the price. I didn't believe him.

Sammy gave me his address and told me to visit him on my next day off. I went to his house on my next day off. He lived in one of the most affluent neighborhoods in town. As I pulled up to the address, I thought it was a joke. It looked like Beverly Hills. A white, two-story mansion with a four-car garage. Reminded me of Elvis's Graceland.

I got out and knocked on his door. Sammy answered and invited me in. He gave me a tour of the place and it was amazing. Olympic-size swimming pool and full garden covered the backyard. Two maids roamed the premises. We passed by his garage, and he had *five* restored cars. Each one had to be $100,000 easily. I was in awe, but I felt weird too. Uncomfortable anxiety settled in my gut.

This was a guy who screamed when the sodas went up ten cents at the vending machine. Now he's walking around with money to burn. Sammy told me, "I got your Tacoma coming for you." I couldn't believe my ears. How could this be? Sammy explained he "knew people" and he'd been buying cars, restoring them, and selling them for top dollar. I didn't buy it and respectfully declined the offer. I left after an hour, my mind blown. Always follow your gut.

About a month later, I was clocking in and getting my things ready to work the line. Today I was assigned to Lane 2. I grabbed my coffee and bumped into a co-worker. She said, "Hey, Rodriguez, did you hear about Sammy? They raided his house this morning and he was arrested. Guess he was letting loaded cars of dope go through for a while. He's up shit creek with no paddle."

Just like that, Sammy had lost it all. His house, cars, property, all seized. Bank accounts were frozen. Pension and benefits down the toilet. Most of all, he'd lost his freedom. Once you lose your freedom, you're done. You have no say what you do from minute to minute. Last I heard they gave him twenty-five years for drug trafficking. Such a shame.

Balance is not something you find, it's something you create.

—Jana Kingsford

Chapter 13

The Good, the Bad and the Nasty

In 2008, I received my transfer orders to a new station. I would be going to Brownsville port. They had four bridges and staffed about four hundred personnel. It was going to be a huge difference, but I was up for the challenge. Anita worked at Brownsville port, so that was a plus. Another good thing was that I'd be closer to home.

The day I left, an old-timer at Progreso warned me, "It's a whole different world over there, Rodriguez. You'll see." As soon as I landed at Brownsville, I understood immediately what he had said.

One difference I registered immediately was the difference in personnel. At Progreso when I first hired on, they had a total of fourteen personnel. I was one of the first new rookies to have landed there in a while. Most of the staff had been there for years. Working double shifts was common since we were always short-staffed. Six-day work weeks were mandatory. The one day you had off would be Tuesday, Wednesday, or Thursday. You couldn't do much during that time. The schedule was like that for a long time.

Since we were such a small number of personnel, we'd always help each other out. If someone needed a day off, we'd switch. Everybody had different lives, different schedules. We all understood this. Being off on a weekend was a no-go. That was the busiest time at the border. We all worked with what we had.

When I got to Brownsville, I realized that wasn't how it worked there.

At Progreso, we had a few bad apples. Some of these cats didn't like the job and loved creating conflict. It was like their entertainment to create issues with people crossing. One guy didn't like anyone (me included). His name was Fink. In my best words, he was evil. I meant, if there was a "Prick of the Century" award, he'd have been the lifetime recipient. He was always arguing with people crossing for no good reason.

One day that I remember in particular, we were working side by side. He was on Lane 1 while I was on Lane 2. Suddenly, I saw his lane backing up while mine continued to flow. I went over to investigate and asked what the holdup was. He started laughing and said, "This idiot doesn't want to show his ID!"

I told the guy in Spanish to show his ID or he'd be arrested. I wasn't playing games.

He responded in Spanish, "Arrest me then, motherfucker." I slapped the cuffs on him immediately. Then I saw his passenger getting out of the vehicle. A *huge* problem.

First off, the passenger was the biggest Mexican I'd ever seen. He had to be six foot three, 280 pounds of solid mass. He'd have made Arnold Schwarzenegger look like a midget. The dude was on major "swole status."

I started to struggle with the first guy. All I remember next is being hit on the back of my head. I yelled for backup as I was starting to feel dizzy from the blows. I looked up and Fink was back in his lane, just staring at the fiasco. I was pissed!

Thank God backup arrived, and we subdued both men. I was even more pissed that Fink didn't help—especially since it was his lane, not mine.

Something was off about Fink. Years later, in 2014, we learned how demented he was. His wife had filed for divorce. Fink finally snapped and shot his wife to death while their three kids (ages seven to sixteen) were inside the house. We later learned they were scheduled to have a restraining order hearing the following morning. Fink was sentenced to fifty years in prison. Sometimes you just never know what really goes inside one's head.

Once I landed at Brownsville, I got to work at all four bridges: B&M, Gateway, Veterans, and Los Indios. Each of the four bridges had their own personality, their own people. Let me explain.

Los Indios had the most considerate people crossing; usually day shoppers and drinkers.

At B&M, you had the snootier people crossing, a much more affluent crowd. Louis Vuitton and Gucci bags were common around the women.

Veterans Bridge travelers were people who'd cross over daily to work in the U.S. They'd cross back in the evening.

Gateway was filled with mostly merchants crossing, along with people headed to the local plasma center.

It was a trip; I liked it. One thing I saw the most at Brownsville was the busloads of Cubans and other "asylees." We never saw this at Progreso.

One day a guy named Davis approached me while we were on our break. I was grabbing a cup of coffee. It was time for shift bids. In the CBP, it all went by seniority. I knew I was one of the top guys on the list. Unlike Progreso, Brownsville didn't have as many personnel with a lot of tenure. Davis asked me what shift I was bidding for. I told him I wanted shift 4. His eyes opened wide. "Shift 4!" he said loudly. I wondered why.

Davis turned his tone down and smiled at me. He said, "Rodriguez, you don't want to get shift 4. That's one of the shittiest shifts to be on. Nobody told you that?" I told him no and he got me thinking for a minute. Why was he so interested in what shift I wanted? I looked up his time and knew I was over him in seniority by a few years. I had a feeling he wanted shift 4. I knew shift 4 was a "cake job" and he was probably eyeballing it.

I told Davis, "Maybe you're right. I think I'll look at shift 1."

Immediately he got a Kool-Aid smile plastered on his face. "Rodriguez, you're an action type of dude. Shift 4 would put grey hair on you faster than you want. You'll love shift 1." He patted me on the shoulder and walked away. As soon as he left, I submitted my papers for shift 4.

One week later, shift bids were announced. They announced them in a room loud and clear. "Rodriguez, Raul. Where you at?"

I raised my hand and shouted to the Officer in Charge "Here, sir!"

The officer in charge replied, "Shift 4 is yours."

I remember looking across the room. There was Davis staring straight at me. He looked like someone had just walked over his nuts. I could see his face had gone pale. When I walked outside to smoke, Davis was right behind me. I turned around and asked him if he was okay. He grabbed his head with both hands and then yelled, "You fucked me, Rodriguez!"

"How?" I asked. "What did I do that has set you off, Davis? I don't understand."

Davis screamed, "You knew I wanted that fucking shift and you stole it from me!"

I pointed out that he had tried to backstab me by telling me shift 4 sucked ass. He never expressed any interest in shift 4 to me. He was only hoping I didn't put in for it because he must've known I had more tenure than he did. I told him, "Let this be a lesson not to fuck people over. It always comes full circle."

He walked away with his shoulder slumped, mumbling curse words to himself. The treachery here was unreal. Nothing like Progreso. As he reached the door, I couldn't help it. "Hey, Davis! I'll let you know how Shift 4 goes!"

He flipped me the bird and slammed the door behind him.

Moonlight is the smuggler's enemy.

—Unknown

Chapter 14

Okies on the Horizon

Brownsville stayed super busy as usual. I worked at all four bridges and, as I said, each one had its own personality. You could tell who belonged and who didn't. The people crossing usually had a purpose and knew where they were going. Then some stood out like a sore thumb.

One day I was working at the Los Indios gate. I saw a nice Ford dually truck rolling up to my lane. The reason it caught my eye was how dirty the truck was. It was carrying two white girls and one white guy. My sixth sense went off. Something looked off.

You check many things when a vehicle rolls up to your lane. You check to see if everyone makes eye contact, if they're too talkative, nervous, and so forth. It's always one of these signs that gives them away. Once this truck pulled up, I got that feeling in my gut. I knew something wasn't kosher.

The truck pulled up and I could see all three occupants staring right at me. The guy wore a trucker's hat, and the two women had cowboy hats on. They were wearing short shorts like Daisy from the show *Dukes of Hazzard*. The guy dressed like a typical cowboy. The first words out of the guy's mouth were "U.S. citizen." I hadn't even asked that yet. I could tell the guy was nervous.

I asked the ladies, and they said the same thing: "U.S. citizen." I asked the group what they were doing in Mexico. The guy explained they had gone down there to party. He was so happy he even showed me an empty bottle of Hornitos Tequila he'd kept. They all told me they had a blast. I asked them where they were from. The guy proudly said "Oklahoma." *Oklahoma?* I knew that was odd.

I asked them how long they'd been down there. They said just one day—another red flag. Are you going to drive 700 miles (typically an eleven-hour drive) from Oklahoma for *one day* of fun? This didn't jive with me at all. The more I kept asking questions, the more their stories came apart. I continued my investigation.

The group was at Los Indios bridge with me. I asked them why they hadn't used another closer bridge like B&M, which was closer to where they supposedly spent their day. Los Indios was mainly agricultural people crossing. It didn't make sense. When I asked the driver why the truck was so muddy, he said he'd crossed through a creek nearby. There wasn't a muddy creek around for miles. I grew more suspicious.

I told the group that I was going to check around the truck. The ladies started touching each other in a sexual way while I was talking with them. They were laughing and making loud noises. They were trying to stop me from looking. But what I hadn't stopped studying was the driver's hands on the steering wheel. He was white knuckling the shit out of that thing. I knew I had something here.

I did my usual checks around the truck. My gut was telling me to check the tires. On a dually truck, two tires are on each of the backsides, the inside tire and the outside tire. I hit the outside tire, and it bounced just as a typical tire should do. The inside tire was a different story. When I tapped the inside tire, I heard a loud thud. No bounce to it. That was it.

I played it cool and acted like I'd found nothing. I went back to the driver and said, "Looks all good here." They all got excited and happy. Then I said, "By the way, do you mind going into the secondary lane? Just doing random checks."

Their lives drained right out of them at that moment. Their happiness vaporized in the wind in one second, flat.

Once we got to the secondary lane, I radioed in for assistance. A buddy of mine named Fuentes came up. I told him, *"Llantas,"* which is Spanish for tires. The group was escorted inside by another agent. Fuentes, a few other agents and I went to work. We started our search and stripped off the tires. A few checks and others agreed with my findings.

While others were peeling the tires apart, we searched for more. I heard an agent who was stripping a tire yell, "Bingo! We got bricks!" I could see the bricks being pulled out of the tires. I felt good about that; I knew my shit. They had given off the wrong feeling.

We pulled a total of fifty bricks of marijuana. The truck was fully loaded. Fuentes came up and told me, "Rodriguez, you da man. You knew it from the jump!"

The group was immediately handcuffed. I went back to the detention unit and saw all three in a cell. They were bawling their eyes out. All the happiness and laughter were gone. Their lives as they knew them were about to change for the worse. They were amateurs when it came to crossing the border. They had no clue.

———

A word to the wise: When crossing the border, at least have your stories straight. Ha!

To stop the importation of drugs
into the U.S.A. is an impossibility.

—George Jung

Chapter 15

Strapped

As the years went on, I continued to witness many changes in the department. Every single one was worthless. They didn't make any sense, and work conditions were at an all-time low. One simple bust or person detained became a three-to-four-hour ordeal. Usually, that would take all of thirty minutes, if that.

I remember one particular incident in 2013 very well.

I was working at the B&M bridge, and a car came down my lane. I could see three passengers; two males and one female. The female passenger, sitting in the front, was a heavy-set lady. I remember the two males had been apprehended previously; I believed it was for smuggling dope. I ran their IDs and, sure enough, they'd been busted in 2010. Some faces you never forget.

One thing I noticed about the lady was that she was very nervous. The guys acted relaxed and were laughing the whole time. They were probably trying to throw me off and get my attention away from the lady. No dice; I sent them to the secondary lane for further inspection. I called for a female officer to assist. I knew this lady was carrying something.

Once in the secondary lane, the guys were searched and led to the "bullpen." That was where we kept detainees who were processing in or out. My female co-worker, Diana, asked the lady if she had anything illegal on her person. The lady said no, and Diana began a pat down on her. Immediately I heard

Diana say loudly, "Que es eso?" That's Spanish for "What's this?" The lady started sobbing.

Mind you, the lady was over three hundred pounds and wearing a muumuu dress. Once the wind blew, I could see her dress lift and see tape strapped around her. Diana and a few other officers led her to the private search room. What we discovered was something we didn't expect to see.

Not only did this lady have two kilos of cocaine strapped to her chest, but she had also more. Diana told us later when she asked her to remove her bra, four more rolled up packages of cocaine fell out. I mean, this lady had done a horrible job hiding this. As she was being led to the bullpen, I heard her screaming for help for her and for her two sons. They were already getting processed and away from her view.

Now came the undaunting task of processing these people. I thanked Diana for her help. She smirked and said, "Have fun processing these three, Rodriguez." Nobody looked forward to this shit. All said and done, the lady was carrying 3.3 pounds of cocaine—street value around $70,000. Four hours later, I got through the processing and went home.

The only reason why it went faster is that two of the three already had records with us. But it was a slow process because the system was constantly crashing. Every page you typed in, you had to save it. If you decided not to and it crashed, you had to start the whole process over. We were working with prehistoric garbage when it came to computers.

It amazed me how shitty our systems were. Mexico had better systems than we did. There is a misconception that the U.S. has the best equipment anywhere. Military, law enforcement agencies, and so forth. That's a total fallacy. What the U.S. does do is send out the best shit to other foreign countries to look good, in my opinion. All for show. Meanwhile, Americans have the hand-me-down type shit to deal with. It's crazy, but these are the facts.

Staff shortages were taking their toll on me. I'd work double shifts weekly and always was angry. I had become an angry, miserable person. Anita and the kids avoided me a lot due to my asshole attitude. I didn't blame them; I hated being in the presence of myself too. Nothing was getting better. The turnover rate at the job was high. Nobody wanted to deal with all this bullshit.

I remember Anita coming into the living room. I was watching TV, but I was mostly staring into an unknown abyss. She snapped me out of my daze. "Raul, are you listening to me?" I asked her what I'd missed. She just shook her head. She told me she hoped I would start to change. I wasn't being the man she had married.

She was right. I was miserable, hated life, hated the fucking job, and hated myself. I was looking to be a better dad, a better husband, a better friend. I asked Anita what she suggested. She said, "Why don't you pray?"

Healing is an art. It takes time, practice, and love.

—Maza Dohta

Chapter 16

Praying for Patience

It was 2014 and things kept going downhill for me. Working double shifts all the time wore me down. Anita and I couldn't plan shit with the kids since we were always at work. I believed that spending time together was the key to building a strong foundation at the house. Little did I know I was doing things totally backwards. I'd being praying—in fact, *begging*—for patience. Sometimes you gotta be careful what you ask for. I'd soon find out the hard way.

One week, I worked five double shifts. I was wiped out after this. I became sick and stayed in bed for two days. I was wondering if I caught a virus. I went to the ER, and they said it was probably just a pinched nerve. I went home with some medicine and that was that. The next day, I couldn't move. I was paralyzed from the neck down. My mind shifted into automatic panic. This couldn't be happening to me.

Anita rushed me to the hospital, and I went into an immediate battery of tests. Suddenly, I was being admitted into the ICU (Intensive Care Unit). *What the fuck is happening?* I couldn't grasp what the problem was.

The doctor came in and talked to us. He said this clearcut and direct: "There's a fifty-fifty chance you make it overnight. I'd have your loved ones come and see you before the day's over."

You've got to be kidding me! Here I am working my ass off to provide for my family. Now this doctor is telling me tonight was possibly my last night on earth. I couldn't move, couldn't think straight, but I knew what was happening. I looked at Anita and said, "I'm fucked." Instantly my life flashed before me. I had short-changed Anita, my kids, even myself. And there I was, possibly living my last day. I started to think, *What have I done here on earth?* I knew I had more to do, but now I was possibly headed out the door. Everything rushed to my head, and I was brain fried. *This may be it,* I thought.

I woke up the next morning to a surprise. Anita and the kids were there and were happy to see me awake. I wanted to know what had happened. I was so groggy and couldn't see straight. The doctor walked in and was excited. "How are you feeling Mr. Rodriguez?"

Stupid question, I thought. How did I feel? I felt like shit and couldn't move my limbs.

The doctor explained to me that I had contracted a thing called GBS (Guillain Barre Syndrome). He said it's a rare neurological disorder in which a person's immune system attacks the peripheral nervous system mistakenly. The peripheral nervous system is the network that carries signals from the brain and spinal cord to the rest of your body. This didn't sound good. One in 100,000 people get this.

He told me that they'd be putting braces on my legs and arms. I didn't want to lay in bed and have my muscles atrophy. Once you stop using them, they basically vaporize. That's when simple movements become much harder. I would be in a wheelchair for moving in the house. I looked like a young Forrest Gump except I had braces on my arms too. That was it.

"Mr. Rodriguez," the doctor said, "you're going to need a lot of patience, a lot of rest."

Those were two things I didn't want to hear. I've always been on the move, ever since I was a kid. It's like being in a Ferrari hauling ass at 180 miles per hour minimum. Now they're telling me the engine blew and I need to go to the waiting room till the engine's fixed—which might take *years*.

Hell no! I never stayed put. Not me. I started to lose my mind. But there were more humiliating things headed in my direction.

Once I lost my basic movements, I needed help with everything. That included going to the bathroom. If you ever had to experience this, it's absolutely the worst. You basically must leave your dignity at the door. There's no way around it. Having an orderly wiping your ass after you took a dump is something I don't wish on anyone, especially a stranger. I've been wiping my ass since I was a kid. Now I am a grown adult, and I need help. I told Anita that wasn't going to happen again. I came up with a brilliant idea.

I told Anita I'd wait to take a dump until she got off work. She was usually at the hospital visiting me by 5:00 p.m. I could do this. No other stranger was going to do that to me. Although it was uncomfortable, I knew Anita well; she knew me. She was my loving wife who'd do anything for me.

When the time came, she pulled through like a champ. Me, on the other hand, I cried inside, full of shame. It's the simple shit that we take for granted. Sitting there in my wheelchair I was determined not to go out ass backwards. If I had a fighting chance, I was going to pull through this. I would become more involved with my family instead of a job that'd replace me in a heartbeat.

———

Once I got home, things became more real. I became a worm and would slide off my wheelchair to get to certain areas. When the kids and Anta were there, no problem. When I was solo, it was different. Plus, any movement I made was progress to me. Hearing the doctor tell me I'd walk correctly in four to five years "if I was lucky" rang in my head constantly. I was determined to get my limbs moving again.

My family started putting me in a rocking chair. I'd rock back and forth for hours tapping my toes on the floor. It must've been annoying to hear this noise, but I was trying to wake up my limbs. In a few weeks, I could feel my toes moving. Progress? Hell yeah! I don't care what any doctor says. Your fight inside will tell you how you're going to progress or fail. I vowed to make it back.

In total, I was out of the job for six months. Within *one* year I was walking correctly again. I wanted to see that doctor again to ask him, "What do you think now?" Never let someone else determine your future or your mindset. They go off charts, graphs, and symptoms. I was banking on my mind and fire in my ass to beat this. Although it was through the grace of God, in my opinion, I sure didn't appreciate him when I was ill. Now, instead of cursing the Lord, I praise him highly. I must remember that he works at his pace, not ours.

———

Work wasn't the same after all this. I really wasn't as motivated as before. I still worked hard but it was different now. Nothing had changed, and things kept moving like clockwork while I was away. We often make the mistake (like I did) of putting everything into a job, a job that'll clip you in a minute for nothing.

Meanwhile, our families who love and care about us get the leftovers. It should be the other way around. I was set on getting there. I owed them that. Most of all, I owed it to myself. Happiness is what I wanted to bathe in. I didn't want to be the pessimistic prick who everyone wanted to avoid. Change was on the way. I was hellbent on making that shift.

The time I spent with Anita and the kids felt golden. It revived me. Fuck the job. That's just what it was: a job. My family was my blood, my reason to wake up and push hard, to provide. They'd never go through the hell I did as a kid. I made that promise to them early on that I wouldn't fail them. Or Anita. They deserved that. They deserved the best I could give them.

Life is really simple, but we insist on making it complicated.

—Confucius

Chapter 17

Hittin' the Crossroads

In 2013, a year before my life-changing illness, my beloved mom, Francisca, passed away. I remember she'd always talk about living your best life. Sometimes she'd tell me I was too stressed out and needed to relax. I guess she could predict my future. Who knows?

When my brother Rene phoned me about her passing, I was heartbroken. She was such an amazing woman. I had to go back to our small town in Matamoros.

Just one problem. I didn't know if it would be safe enough, but I couldn't miss this.

In our small ranch town outside Matamoros, everyone knew when an outsider touched down. Nobody kept secrets there, and everyone's eyeballs were wide open. I knew our town was still a dumping ground for deceased cartel members. It had been that way since I was a kid. For fun in our childhood, we'd go hunting for dead bodies. A few times we struck gold too. It was the norm for us. Now, being grown up and a federal officer of the CBP, this posed a problem.

I told my brother Rene my concerns but that I was headed that way regardless. He told me there weren't going to be any cartel members around. I had to take his word for it on this one. I'd done plenty of damage to the cartel organizations throughout my career. Now I was headed straight into the lion's den with no arms or anything to defend myself. I braced for the worst. I had no choice.

Once I arrived at our parents' house, I was greeted by many family members. I recognized a few familiar faces and was happy to see old friends. I loved being there. It was the one place that always felt like home to me. Plus, we'd helped fix up our parents' house over the years.

Mind you, when we were kids, we had no running water and no electricity. Floors were flat dirt. No bathroom, only an outhouse behind our shed. During the years to come, we'd help get electricity installed in the house. Running water was the next. A new rooftop and a septic tank for a new bathroom. I wanted our parents to live better. Everyone who could do so chipped in with money and/or labor. It was great to know we'd all helped.

As a family, we started to get all the affairs for the funeral in order. I saw two familiar faces running around, filling up coolers with drinks, throwing the trash out, and anything else they could do to help. I asked my brother who they were. He responded, "That's Lalo and Mauri." Oh yes, I remembered them; they were an old friend's two youngest sons. They were around nineteen to twenty-one years old when I arrived there. These guys were hauling ass and were a big help.

Throughout this whole three-day visit, I was always looking over my shoulders. I knew for a fact everyone knew who I was and what I did for a living. Mauri had seen me looking over towards the road. He startled me and told me in Spanish, "You don't need to worry, Raul. You're covered."

It must've shown on my face. You've got to remember, I didn't want to end up in the dumping grounds. Or hanging from a bridge at the town's entrance. Many times, this had happened throughout Mexican states. Snagging a federal officer would be a gold bar for these criminal organizations. I had to be aware of my surroundings.

After three days, we were done. We'd done the viewing, the funeral, and the mass. It was a hard time, but we pulled together as family. I saw Lalo and Mauri packing up some chairs onto their little pickup truck. They had done an exceptional job helping us out. Many of the town locals had attended my mom's services; she was well-liked and always helped people out in town.

The healthcare over in Matamoros and our little town was expensive. Most couldn't afford medical care. My mom would come up with ancient remedies to handle any medical issue that arose. She'd handle things like a girl's first period, stomach issues, fever symptoms, whatever. She did family planning for many in our town. I can always recall our house being full of people, all seeking medical treatment or life advice. Mom was amazing.

I told Rene that Lalo and Mauri had helped so much. I was more surprised that no cartel members had come around to investigate. Rene jumped in fast and said, "Well, Raul, I didn't want to alarm you, but Lalo and Mauri work for one of these criminal organizations. I had spoken with them about you before you even came down. The coast was clear. You got a pass."

I didn't believe him at first. I couldn't understand why they'd done me a solid like that. My only thought was, maybe they had that much love and respect for my mom. They probably wanted to keep things chill. Either way, I respected Lalo and Mauri for this. About the time I had recovered from my illness, I asked Rene about the two. Rene had told me they were ambushed on the outskirts of town, machine-gunned to death. That's life for a criminal/cartel member. They start them off young, and they die even quicker. I was sad to hear this news.

Pivoting isn't Plan B. It's part of the process.

—Jeff Goins

Chapter 18

Shifting Gears

By 2016, I had hit a wall when it came to work. It wasn't the same anymore. The changes that came never turned out for the better. The younger the recruits who came in, the more people had an "I don't care" mentality. I transferred to the cargo lane, which was better. Los Indios and Veterans bridges only had cargo lanes for the semi-trucks to roll through. This position came with a big perk.

When you're on a regular lane, you're never inside the booth. You're constantly checking cars, looking to see the passengers, and observing the vehicles. It's always hot and humid outside.

When you work on the cargo lanes, you never leave the booth. I transferred here since I was on light duty after my illness. It was a great move on my part. The reason you don't leave the booth is because the semi-trucks go through an X-ray that's raised up. The common place to find drugs or any type of contraband on a semi-truck is the front of the trailer. Most smugglers believe that we won't unload the whole trailer since it's a painstaking process.

That's where smugglers are wrong. We unloaded many trucks loaded to the gills. They were almost always loaded in the front. It usually took us an hour to easily pull all the pallets of goods out. Then we'd discover the contraband. When we arrested the drivers, usually they played the "I'm just a truck driver" bit. They always knew what they were carrying. They got paid extremely well by the drug organizations if they got through.

I've been asked many times by people who don't work for CBP if we catch all the drugs/contraband going through our borders. The answer is simple: Hell no! Let's say we catch a semi-truck loaded with drugs. While ten officers unload the cargo and tie up in the secondary, ten more trucks are passing by, loaded. You probably catch 10 percent if you're lucky. There's no way to stop the flow of it.

Like I said before, the war on drugs has been an epic failure for more than four decades now. We'd never be able to plug up that line if we tried.

Another big issue, I believe, is that our own government flies this shit in and funnels it into poor minority cities. Just like in the '80s, when they flooded South Central Los Angeles with crack cocaine. It's a joke.

My attitude towards the job had changed. I started doing different things outside of work.

Anita, the kids, and I had started taking vacations out of the city more. We'd travel to places like New Orleans, Tennessee, and other locations. Most people who grow up in the Valley never leave the place. I wanted our kids to see more of the country. Some places you liked and some places you never wanted to revisit. It's better to see and experience this all.

Back at the job, we had a chief in charge of the cargo lanes named Hero. To be honest, he was a complete asshole. He always wanted to find a flaw of yours or something you did wrong. I think he was envious of us seasoned vets on the job since we had more experience. Plus, a lot of us read up on the laws constantly.

One day I encountered this truck I suspected of being loaded. My lane was busy, and I second guessed myself. It happens. So, I let the truck go through. About three hours later, here comes Hero charging up to my booth. I could see he had a smirk on his face. I must've done something wrong. That's the only time you ever saw Hero, when you fucked up.

"Rodriguez, do you know you let a loaded truck go through? They caught it at the checkpoint fifty miles away." I knew which truck it was and asked Hero to confirm. He verified. I knew it; I'd had a feeling it was loaded.

Hero continued ranting and let me know I had to be more vigilant when observing trucks. I offered him the opportunity to jump in my booth with me to show off his perfectionist skills. Of course, he declined and stormed off.

Everybody in any career makes mistakes. It's funny to see people like Hero who think they know more than anyone. Just to fuck with him, I'd ask him about certain immigration laws. He'd always come up with an excuse and never answered me. He'd walk off. That's because he didn't know the laws like some of us did.

My game came from my mentor Jose Trevino. That guy was a wizard when it came to laws. He was a grumpy old man who chained smoked like a chimney. He had one of those rough voices and a harsh tone. Nobody wanted to converse with him much, but I did. He was constantly pounding into my head, "Rodriguez, read those damn immigration laws. Knowledge is *power*. The more you know, the more valuable you become."

Back in the early part of my career, we had to read these massive books page by page. It was worse than a lawyer trying to locate a case in a law library. Nowadays, everything is computerized. Nobody has to search the books for anything, yet they still don't utilize the online resource.

The younger generation of workers at CBP were straight *huevóns*. (That's Spanish for "lazy.") They had no respect for the public at all. They tried to act like some badass detectives. We used to laugh and call these guys "supercops." It was funny to watch but, at the same time, sad. They had no drive in them whatsoever. I was always telling Anita I couldn't wait for the day I was retired. I wanted to just be at home, raising our children and farm animals. Our animals always brought me peace. Much more than any human could bring.

I told Anita I needed to see what the status was for my brother Rene. Since I was an American citizen, I wanted to get Rene a green card through me. He'd always wanted to come over and it would be great for him to have that chance. Plus, we did it the legal way. Anita told me to get his application going. She said to reapply if nothing happened. What else could go wrong, right? All they could do was say no. Little did I know that this simple process was going to flip my world upside down. I had no clue what was ahead of me. None.

Yesterday is ours to recover,
but tomorrow is ours to win or lose.

—Lyndon B. Johnson

Chapter 19

The Application

I applied for my brother Rene's visa in 2005. I updated our status around 2016. Still nothing, but as I said before, this is a long, drawn-out process. If you don't have a lawyer helping, the effort's going to take years. I had been getting worried since it had been more than thirteen years now. I inquired about Rene's visa but to no avail. It was always the same "It's in process" line. I swear, that's all the administrative people are allowed to say.

During my time at CBP, we'd get random drug tests. It was mandatory and I never worried about that since I never used drugs. I was always one of those guys who could have a few beers at home and be good. I didn't have to get smashed and reckless. I did enough of that shit when I was in the Navy.

We'd also get background checks done every five years. They'd see if you have any criminal or negligent charges against you. Not everyone who gets busted goes and rats himself out to his boss. They must do their due diligence and make sure everyone is on the up and up. It's part of the job.

Rene gave me a call one day asking about his status. I had told him nothing had changed yet. There are immigrant visas and tourist visas; he wanted to get a full visa with no time limit. A green card. Immigrant visas are given to people who are allowed to come to the U.S. to live and work. A tourist visa is given for ten years and lets them come back for a few months at a time. He's the only one of my siblings who wished to live in the U.S.

The U.S. allots a certain number of visas each year. Mexico has the most allotted because they have the most applicants. Once those numbers are reached, other applicants must wait for the next year. This is why the process drags, and most people get too frustrated to wait. A lot end up crossing illegally unfortunately.

Corruption is always a problem in CBP and other agencies as well. Keep in mind that the criminal organizations in Mexico aren't short on cash. They can pay you a year's salary if you let one truck go across loaded with drugs. Many people end up taking the bait. Once you do one thing for these organizations, you're trapped. No way out of it.

I remember around this time a group of six CBP agents came by the lunchroom. One of them was a cocky Mexican called Benito. Benito and his crew would always be inviting me to Matamoros on Wednesdays. They said they crossed over to go watch live wrestling and get drunk.

I kept telling Benito over and over, "No thanks." One day he sat down next to me and said, "Why don't you come with us, Raulito? You'll have a blast with us." I told him he'd have to be nuts to cross over to Matamoros. If a cartel caught us, our heads would be coming off. Plus, I told him wrestling was so fake. I didn't need to go to bars to have a good time. I loved being at home with Anita and the kids. I had animals I needed to tend to daily. Go out drinking? Nah, I'm good.

Benito told me they were covered. They have no problem with the cartels, and they got a "pass." Something told me in my gut they were up to nefarious activities over the border. I wanted no part of that shit. Finally, Benito gave up. He stood up and told the others he thought I was gay; that's why I didn't want to hang with them in Mexico.

That was all I could take. I told Benito he had crossed a line and to get out of my face. He looked stunned and said, "We just want you to join us, Raulito. Don't be a square."

I told him and his crew I didn't need to prove shit to anybody. I stormed out of the lunchroom and told Anita that night that they were up to no good. I was right.

A week later, I was heating up my food in the lunchroom. I was by myself until Ceci, one of our managers, came in. Ceci was a seasoned agent and rose through the ranks faster than me. She was someone whom I respected; she had a lot of knowledge. She closed the door and looked around. She asked me if Benito and his crew had asked me to do anything illegal.

I told her no, and that Benito was a pain in the ass. I was honest with her about my feelings and told her I didn't care to hang with that bunch. Plus, I told her that something was off about him. She asked me why I thought that. I told her that they'd been inviting me to Matamoros every Wednesday to go drinking. I told her I declined and didn't want to be a part of that.

Ceci locked the door and spoke in a very low voice, saying, "Raul, stay away from that bunch. They're conducting a huge investigation on Benito and his crew. Don't go anywhere near them. That's the best advice I can give you."

She unlocked the door and walked out. I knew what she meant. Usually when someone is being investigated, ten out of ten go to jail. I give her props for telling me about this. Ceci could lose her job if I opened my mouth.

I'd never do that though. I wasn't raised to be a snitch. Plus, I didn't have anything to worry about. I wasn't doing anything illegal. I did my job and did the best I could—always for my family.

About a month later, I was passing the manager's office when I saw Benito come out. He wasn't smiling this time. He had a piece of paper in his hand. He nodded at me and walked out of the building. I heard later that Benito and a few others were allowed to resign. One of the five was arrested. I heard they were never busted red-handed but were let go due to affiliation with a cartel attorney. This attorney had funded them with gifts, all-expense paid trips, and money. I remember telling myself at that moment, *I'll never be in the hot seat at that office.* Little did I know, I'd be there and in deep shit soon. Very soon.

Sometimes life is going to hit you in the head with a brick.
Don't lose faith.

—Steve Jobs

Chapter 20

The Walk of Shame

April 18, 2018, is a day I will never forget. I was having a great morning. I had slept well, had my coffee in my thermos, and carried a great packed lunch. I made my way over to the Los Indios gate. I started to get settled into my lane. Before I could do any of that, I heard my co-worker Ramon yell, "They want you in the office, Raulito."

I closed my lane and went inside to see what was going on. I thought, *Shit, mandatory overtime, I bet.* I was so far off this time. I walked into the manager's office thinking, *More overtime. Great. I guess it's part of the job.*

When the door opened, two of my managers, Rita and Seth, walked in. I respected them a lot and waited to hear the news. I sensed something was wrong. Rita and I were usually cool. Now she had a look on her face like someone had walked over her grave.

"Mr. Rodriguez, can you read this please?" She handed me a white envelope.

I opened it up and was nearly knocked off my chair. It read, "You are being placed under criminal investigation." I couldn't believe this. "What the hell is going on?" I asked Rita.

She said I would have to give up my credentials, my badge, my gun, everything. I was blindsided. I couldn't believe this. I had done nothing wrong or illegal. My mind started to race.

After being stripped of basically everything I had worked for the last eighteen years, I sat down and couldn't think straight. Rita told me that they would be contacting me soon about my case. She could not divulge any more.

Holy shit! I had no clue what this was about. As soon as I walked out of the manager's office, I immediately saw people staring at me. It was the longest walk I had ever taken out of that building. Everyone could see that I had no gun belt, no badge, no nothing. I could hear snickers and whispers of "What did he get busted for?" and "Fucking traitor." It was a walk of shame, and I had no idea why. I was baffled like everyone else. I didn't say shit and walked out to my car. I left Anita a message to call me ASAP. She called me a few minutes later.

I screamed on the phone to Anita, "Can you believe I'm under criminal investigation? They took all my credentials, badge, gun, everything!"

I was pissed. Reality was setting in. I knew I was clear of whatever they were accusing me of. Maybe Valles had thrown my name around to be an ass. I had a thousand thoughts rushing to my brain.

Anita calmed me down and told me we'd figure this out. I still had absolutely no idea what lay ahead of me—*zero!*

The next day, Seth called me and told me to report to Gateway bridge Monday morning. He advised me not to show up in uniform. I'd be placed on administrative duties. Basically, a desk jockey. This wasn't for me at all.

For the next three days, I sat at a desk with nothing to do. I was reading on my phone and on the internet to kill time, and that was all I did. Since I didn't have my credentials, I couldn't get into the computer. I couldn't check e-mails, send out forms, or anything else.

I hit my max and called my Union steward over; we'll call him "Jerry." He was a young, white guy who was one of my mentees. I'd given him a lot of knowledge and showed him the ropes. Now it was my ass on the ropes. Circumstances changed so fast.

"Jerry, I can't sit here anymore. Can I just use up my sick leave and vacation days till this mess is cleared up?" He agreed, and I took off. I was not going to linger in an office doing nothing. Plus, I had over a year's worth of time accrued so I wasn't worried. I could outlast this—or so I thought. I'd find out later it was much bigger than I could've imagined.

The following week I was called back to the office by the OIG (the Office of the Inspector General). This is where all the criminal cases went. As I walked in, it reminded me of a big, interrogation room. Two-way mirrors, microphone recording setup, the works. I sat down next to Jerry who was representing me as my Union steward. A man and woman from the OIG office walked in. The woman had a manila envelope and slid it to me across the table. "You recognize this, Mr. Rodriguez?"

I opened the envelope and discovered a Mexican birth certificate. It had my name on it, my parents' names, my grandparents' name. My birthdate was given as 10/26/68. My U.S. birth certificate indicated my birthdate was 1/14/69, the birthday I'd always used.

It all made sense now. I knew exactly what this meant. I'd been living a lie and only one person could explain this: my dad.

I was livid, yet I sat there paralyzed and in shock. I kept staring at that Mexican birth certificate. I felt my career shattering like a glass bottle on rocks. All my life, I'd done the right things for the most part. I taught my kids to do the same. I worked hard, and when I got tired, I worked even harder. Now all this is going down the garbage chute for some reason I had no clue about. My sadness quickly turned to heated anger. I asked Jerry and the two OIG officials if I could call my dad to meet. They would not leave my sight and hold my phone. I wanted to clear the air in front of them all. They were shocked and agreed.

I called my nephew, Tomas. I told him, "Get your grandfather and tell him to meet me at the local Starbucks off the highway. *Do not* tell him why, just to meet me there. Call me back immediately and I mean *immediately.*"

I was going to prove my innocence hell or high water. Tomas called back ten minutes later. "We'll be leaving the house in five minutes."

Good. I hung up and handed my phone to Jerry. All four of us loaded up in a vehicle. On our way to prove my innocence: at Starbucks!

Don't lie about anything, ever. Lying leads to hell.

—Jordan Peterson

Chapter 21

A Day of Reckoning

The drive to Starbucks was a drag. Even though we were only fifteen minutes away, I wanted to be there immediately. I felt like telling the agent who was driving to *step on it*. I had no worries because I knew I was innocent. I wanted to confront my dad and get this shit straightened.

We arrived at Starbucks and entered the building. The agents and Jerry took a seat at the table. I greeted my nephew and thanked him for bringing my dad. This meeting was crucial. It was my ass on the line, and I wanted the agents to hear the facts.

The agents slid a copy of my Mexican birth certificate to my dad, and they asked him firmly, "Where was Raul Rodriguez born?"

Dad quickly responded, "In the United States." He looked befuddled as to what was going on. I could see in his eyes he looked nervous. I couldn't take it anymore, so I told my Dad to tell them the truth. My whole career was on the line.

He lowered his head and stared at the floor. He uttered softly, "He was born in Mexico."

That was it. I was rocked to the core when I heard it. I felt my heart drop out of my torso and slam on the bottom of my feet. I knew right then and there, *You're fucked, Raul*. That's all I could think. An impeccable CBP career, flushed down the fucking toilet. I was so pissed it became sickening.

A Government Secret

The agents looked at each other just dumbfounded. Jerry looked surprised too. They all could see I had been telling the truth, not knowing any of this mess. If I had known this, I would've fixed this mess the legal way. Now I was at the mercy of the U.S. government—not a good predicament to be in.

Dad spoke up, telling the agents, "Please, Raul had no idea of this. It wasn't his fault. He never knew anything about this." In my head I thought, too late for that shit. I'm screwed.

Right after that, one of the agents turned to me and said, "You're cleared. There will be no criminal charges brought against you, Raul. It's clear to us you had no clue about this birth certificate. Now it's up to the CBP what they want to do on the administrative side."

Cool, I thought. I felt a little better thinking they would have my back. Plus, I had the union on my side too.

OFFICE OF INSPECTOR GENERAL
Department of Homeland Security

Washington, DC 20528   www.oig.dhs.gov

REPORT OF INVESTIGATION

Case Number:	
Case Title:	Raul Rodriguez Customs and Border Protection Officer GS-12 U.S. Customs and Border Protection Brownsville, Texas
Report Status:	Final
Alleged Violation(s):	18 USC 1001~ False Statements, Entries, or Concealing or Covering Up A Material Fact

SYNOPSIS

This investigation was initiated based upon receipt of information from U.S. Citizenship and Immigration Services (USCIS) which stated that an Overseas Verification (OVR) regarding the U.S. birth certificate for Raul Rodriguez (R. Rodriguez), U.S. Customs and Border Protection Officer (CBPO), Brownsville, Texas, resulted in the discovery of a Mexican birth certificate for R. Rodriguez, which pre-dated the U.S. birth certificate which was registered by a convicted midwife.

The Department of Homeland Security (DHS), Office Inspector General (OIG) investigation included reviewing records submitted by USCIS, review of Mexican and U.S. birth certificates, and interviews of R. Rodriguez and R. Rodriguez' father. The facts collected failed to substantiate the allegation that R. Rodriguez knowingly submitted a fraudulent U.S. birth certificate in an attempt to adjust the immigration status of his brother.

DHS OIG presented the facts of the investigation to the Assistant United States Attorney's Office, Southern District of Texas, McAllen, Texas, who declined the case for prosecution.

I was still livid with my dad though. I was in this mess because of him. I told the agents that this meeting was adjourned.

I had nothing else to say and wanted to get this all cleared up. I said goodbye to my nephew and thanked him for bringing Dad. My dad, however, didn't say a word. No apology, no goodbye, no nothing. I know he was ashamed but had too much fucking pride to apologize. That pissed me off even more.

I walked outside to find Anita, my youngest son, and daughter waiting for me. I hugged Anita and told her it was true. I was so in shock, I could barely utter the words. My son and daughter were clearly upset. When I heard my daughter say, "Dad's an illegal," I felt like saying, "No, Dad's a fraud. A fraud due to my own father's stupidity."

My son started asking Anita if I would be deported. He was worried I'd get whacked if I ever crossed into Mexico. He wasn't far off on that thought. I couldn't feel a damn thing. I only felt anger and pain. I didn't know what the hell was going to happen to me. I had to regain my composure as my mind was spinning out of control. Anita told me to relax and that we'd get through this. We had options.

The agents had said they would help me out. I was on the fence with that but wanted to trust the process. I'd later find out how dumb it was to even hope. The next two weeks I spent tending to my farm animals and hanging out with my family. I loved being there but was anxious to see how CBP would help me. I would soon find out.

After two weeks, I received a call from ICE (Immigration and Customs Enforcement). One of their lawyers was on the line. He wanted to set up a meeting ASAP. I told him to meet me at my lawyer's office at noon. He agreed. I'd discover quickly how slimy these assholes were.

When I arrived at my lawyer's office, this ICE guy was already there waiting. He smiled and shook my hand firmly.

He acted like my friend.

The ICE guy seemed energetic and told me he had good news for me. The deal was, they would hold my job for three years if I signed a paper saying I wouldn't sue CBP. I told him I had no intention of ending up in court for anything. I just wanted my job back. I needed to go back to work. I hadn't knowingly committed a crime.

He agreed and said there wouldn't be a problem. "Sign right here, Mr. Rodriguez." He slid a piece of paper out of his briefcase and launched a pen across the table. I signed and he smiled from ear to ear. "That's all I have here." He shook my hand and left my lawyer's office, just like that.

You must learn the rules of the game. Then you must play better than anyone else.

—Unknown

Chapter 22

Unknown Status

Once I signed those papers, all went downhill. What ICE did was hand my case over to a judge who had a reputation for hoarding cases. I mean, they couldn't have fucked me any better than this. He was some old geezer who hadn't been in a courtroom for ages. I was told I had three years to get my job back. June 2021 was the deadline.

When three years had passed, I started getting impatient. I was wondering what the hell was going on with my file. Was I going to get my job back or be fired? I needed to know. I'd been following and keeping track of my case for the past three years. Nothing. My status was always the same on the computer: Pending.

June 2021 came finally. Guess what this judge did? He retired and my file was once again in limbo. I couldn't believe my fucking ears! They really knew how to screw with me. If it wasn't for Anita and my kids, I would've lost my shit. What the hell was going on?

My case got handed to a judge in Dallas named Judge Freeman in November 2022. She was a nice lady and told me, off the record, that this was the worst screw job she'd seen in her career. She immediately granted me status without any rights. I could stay in the U.S. until I got my visa. I could still be deported though. But it was progress.

I waited three years while this old geezer judge sat on his ass with no updates or movement. But I couldn't complain; Judge Freeman was a straight up judge. I respected that.

I received an anonymous call from a woman who identified herself as Judy. Since I'd been removed from my job, I'd get a lot of these; it wasn't uncommon. Some were good and some were outright vicious.

Judy explained to me that CBP would probably not take me back. My case was unique, and they hadn't had a case like mine. If they hired me back, it would be a black eye against the agency. They'd had people before who got caught knowingly using falsified documents. In my case, I had no idea my documents were bogus; that was the difference in my case. She told me my chances were slim-to-none, and I should consider the harsh reality of that.

I told her, "Thanks for the info," and hung up. What she said held some water though. I'd already started to think along those lines. But I wasn't built to quit, nor was I going to fold. My whole life, my family, my dignity, my integrity, everything hung on this. I couldn't just accept this as a loss. I didn't have another twenty years to jumpstart a new career. This was my *raison d'etre*. Giving up was *never* an option.

My lawyer advised me to go to the media with my story. He wanted me to gain traction so I could stay and get my citizenship. I agreed it was a smart move. My first interview was with a Spanish television channel named Telemundo. How did it go, you ask? Total disaster, in my opinion. Here's why.

I wasn't used to being in the spotlight. I was never a guy who thrived on attention. I did my job and remained humble, low key. I didn't frequent bars or stray out of my relationship with Anita. I was a family man who loved being home with them. Now this guy who interviewed me hit me with all kinds of questions I wasn't ready for.

I kept stammering and stuttering throughout the interview. I was nervous and the words couldn't fly out of my mouth correctly. I had no other option though. The U.S. government was trying to kill my career and my status. I hadn't knowingly done anything wrong. I was being treated like a convicted murderer on death row. I didn't deserve this. I got a call from a reporter named Jeremy Rath. He worked for a New Jersey newspaper called *The Atlantic.*

Rath wanted to interview me about my story; he found it interesting. I told my lawyer, and he agreed to my getting more attention. My story had to be told. I needed some major help. I agreed with Rath to do the interview. We set up a meeting. My goal was to tell the truth and nothing else. I had nothing to hide. I never did. My career was impeccable. I hoped the CBP and others saw this. All I wanted was to get back to work. I had a family to support.

The saddest thing about betrayal is that it never comes from your enemies.

—Unknown

Chapter 23

Coconuts & Brownies

I started to gain traction and receive calls from various news outlets; not just in the continental United States, but from around the world. Spain, Germany, you name it. I spoke with a few over the phone. I really wanted to gain attention for my case here in the U.S. My lawyer agreed and said, "Any light is good." So, my meeting with Jerry Rath finally came to fruition.

Jerry was a nice guy in my opinion. He spoke eloquently and started asking me all the hard questions. The one question every reporter has *always* asked is, "Raul, you knew you were illegal, right? You can tell me."

This question made me laugh each time I was asked this. I answered Jerry the same way I did everyone else: "Hell no!" I told Jerry if that had been the case, I would've gotten a job as far as possible from the government. I'd be a landscaper working for cash under the table so I wouldn't be found. Or a furniture mover. Not with the CBP, the "Lion's Den." I might've been born at night but not last night. I would've flown under the radar as best as possible. It didn't make sense, and Jerry understood what I meant.

We hung out for two or three weeks. I showed him my house, the animals I tended to, and my daily family life. He wasn't shy about asking me anything, and I wasn't hesitant to answer anything. I think that surprised him a lot. He was thrown off when I told him that growing up, I never wanted to live in the U.S. I was beyond happy in Matamoros.

I told him it was a prison sentence going to the U.S. My only glimmer of hope was reaching summer. I'd be "paroled" out of the hell I was living in Texas every June. Matamoros to me was living. I had my sister Amalia and my siblings with me. My mom was like the town medic/go-to woman. She had a remedy for everything.

Jerry turned the conversation to my dad. Things got really tense during this time. I say "tense" because it's a delicate subject when it comes to him. It really has screwed me up what I went through all those years. Jerry and I were having coffee, and he hit me sideways. "Raul, do you talk to your dad anymore?"

I shot back quickly, "No, that guy is a piece of shit. Look at what I'm going through because of his actions." I won't forget the look Jerry gave me. He was stunned to hear that, I guess. I was being honest with him. Let me explain so you get it.

Jerry and many others hadn't seen the hell I endured. It was my dad who was a drunk, a gambler, and an abuser. You're never the same when you've seen your mom beaten and struggling to feed us. My dad would fuck off or drink his money away. We had nothing because of his drinking and whoring. He made all the decisions in the house. He's the reason my sister Mireya and I were sent away.

I was sent away to my aunt's, where I was tormented daily by my aunt and cousins. You never understand unless you've lived it. I told Jerry that my dad was the cause of this. And now I'm possibly going to be deported forever due to his fuckery.

My anger wasn't about me. What about Anita, the kids? Who was going to support them if they hauled my ass out of here? This is the problem that most people don't understand.

After three weeks of hanging out with me, Jerry departed for home, back to New Jersey. I wished him well and thanked him for his time. He said the article would be out in three months, tops. I was really looking forward to it and hoped people would see I had done nothing wrong. I just wanted to continue with daily life uninterrupted.

About two months later, the article appeared in *The Atlantic*. I was stunned to see what was printed.

Jerry had put out what I said about my dad being a piece of shit. I'd told him that in confidence and was caught up in my emotions at the time. I didn't think he would do that; but then again, satire sells. All the pain I'd endured came out during that interview. But, as of today, my dad is just a broken, old man. Even though he did some real dumb shit and put me into this position, I didn't want to hurt him. I'm sure he regretted what he'd done, though I never heard an apology. His face said it all during that meeting at Starbucks with the agents.

I didn't want to cause him pain. I didn't enjoy that. I thought, if were my kids calling me a piece of shit, I'd be shattered. It was too late though. Once it was printed, the world got to see my interview. Soon enough, the comments below the article came flooding in like a hurricane.

The comments came mostly from fellow Hispanics responding to the article. They were nasty, too. Anita warned me not to look at them, but I couldn't resist. Sure enough, all the comments were blasting me from each direction. Every derogatory word came flying my way.

I was used to being called a "coconut, *vendido*, and whitewashed." A coconut means brown on the outside, white on the inside. A *vendido* means a "sellout or traitor" in Spanish. Some of the comments were, "Good! You deserve to be deported, asshole! This is what you get mf for deporting your own people, you ungrateful bastard! How can you speak about your dad like that?"

You get the hint now, right?

A Government Secret

The common comment was, "How could you deport your own people for years and now cry like a woman?"

Here's my response to this. It's never changed.

Every country has immigration laws. Yes, *every* country. To come and live in another country, a person has to follow a correct process for this. Otherwise, many people *not* seeking a better life will ruin it. It's that simple. I was doing my *job*. That's what working for the CBP was all about for me: making a difference and making an honest living so my family never went without whatever they needed.

I never took my job personally. Rules are rules, though. We all must answer someone in life; that's just a fact. I'd ask those same people, "So if I get fired, my family and I can move in with you? You can support us, right?"

The answer was always, "No." Yeah, see that swath, I thought.

I wasn't asking for any favors. I hadn't done anything wrong. I could've gotten citizenship through Anita, but they sunk that possibility fast. The government pulled one out of their ass with their next move. To permanently screw me, they used a case: Zheng vs U.S. It's an old case of an Asian guy who purchased a legit certificate of citizenship from a USCIS official. That same USCIS official was later convicted of selling documents and sent to federal prison.

He was eventually caught and deported. Now they're bringing up this old case to stonewall me. It had *nothing* to do with my case. Absolutely *nothing!* I had never purchased any documents illegally, nor did I have any knowledge of any wrongdoings. As of now, the Zheng case is used to screw others in the same boat as me. It's ludicrous. The comments continued to fly in. I'm used to it now. Once again, back to that "crawdad mentality." We bring our own down the most. It's a tragedy, to be honest.

I'd rather ride down the street on a camel
than give what is sometimes called an in-depth interview.

—Warren Beatty

Chapter 24

The Sit Down with CNN

Around February of 2023, I received a call from a correspondent from CNN (the Cable News Network). Some call it the Communist News Network. I always kept my own opinion to myself and kept an open mind. I needed the world to see what the government was doing to one of their own.

I agreed to see this reporter, Catherine Shoichet. We spoke on the phone, and she agreed to come to San Benito to interview me. Although I was a bit skeptical, I needed my story to be heard. My scream had no voice, and I needed to be heard. I prayed it would all go well.

A few days later, I got a knock on the door. When I opened it, Catherine was standing there, right on time. She struck me as a nerdy, white lady with glasses. She was very welcoming and very cordial. I introduced her to my family, and we began to converse.

Over the next two days, Catherine and I talked about my case. We had so many things to talk about, I didn't even know where to begin. She really set me at ease, and it was a pleasure to talk to her. She couldn't believe the atrocities I had been facing. I told her I lived a life in limbo. It was crazy.

Once we were finished, she wished me well and said goodbye. Once she returned to her office, she called me and set me at ease. She told me that she wouldn't publish the article till I read it and was okay with it. I was happy about this, since I was a little bit on the fence. Jerry Rath had promised the same, yet he published the part of our conversation when I called my dad "a piece of shit." I caught a lot of flak for that. Had Jerry published the real reason *why* I had said that, people would have understood. I got a lot of hate mail and nasty comments for that quote.

Sure enough, once Catherine was done, she sent me her rough draft. To be honest, I was a bit surprised. It wasn't fluffed up with all kinds of extra add-ons. It was exactly what we'd talked about. I gave her the okay, and she advised me it would be published on Sunday for the world to see.

The article was published on Sunday night. I thought it came out perfectly and was pleased with Catherine's efforts towards this. Once it was over, Anita and I began talking about the interview. We were interrupted. My phone started ringing off the hook.

Now, mind you, I had done interviews for German, French, and Spanish newspapers. I had never received so many calls. In fact, I was wondering how the hell everybody had my phone number. I didn't even know how to handle this. Anita and I started scheduling different outlets for interviews. We got requests from Miami, Houston, Univision—you name it.

Once we scheduled our interviews, life was nuts. Most of the time, I'd be doing an interview while two or three other reporters were waiting outside. They were very patient and didn't care if they had to wait their turn. After a few weeks, the noise settled down. I read all the articles the following weeks. I must say, Catherine's article with CNN was the best. She had it uncut and to the point. Other accounts blindsided me like the interview I did with Jerry Rath.

Another article (I refuse to mention the media outlet) I got a lot of heat for was because they had published that I had voted for Trump in 2016. What they didn't explain is why I did. They left that part out.

Let me explain this clearly to you. I stated in this interview why I had voted for Trump. My exact words, when asked why I voted for Trump, were these: "I voted for Trump because he was going to create chaos and bring out all the imperfections of the U.S. government." Period! It had absolutely *nothing* to do with immigration or my case.

Mind you, in 2016, I was still a highly decorated CBP official. Still working for CBP at the time. I know why this was published though. It was to nail me to the cross and act like I was crying now that I was on the other side of the fence. It had nothing to do with that. What blows me away is we supposedly live in a "free country" where people are free to vote for whoever they want. Not the case anymore.

So many people have stopped talking to friends, family members, all because they have a difference in political views. I haven't seen this much division even when it comes to religious beliefs. It's sad yet it's the reality we live in today. If I count have a dollar for every nasty comment I've received along the lines of "Fuck you Rodriguez, you got what you deserved," I'd be retired on an island. Straight facts. This is what "we the people" stand for. Hell no. It's an absolute farse. We're one step away from a Communist dictatorship. These are facts we can no longer sweep under the rug.

Being on tour is like being in limbo.
It's like going from nowhere to nowhere.

—Bob Dylan

Chapter 25

A Man with No Country

The present day brings many new obstacles. With each new day, I cannot stop and wonder if it's my last day in the U.S. It's a feeling that never goes away. I've dedicated my entire life and career to this beloved country. Now I'm on the verge of possibly being deported. If that happens, I'll never be able to come back. I can see that already.

Basically, I'm a man with no country. My flag is unknown now as I cannot be classified as a U.S. citizen. I see a lot of people (mainly Latinos) who want to see me deported. It's crazy when you think about it. Haven't we learned by now that the "crawdad mentality" has got us nowhere. It just keeps on going.

I lived a lie for the first 49 years of my life. From what I'd been told, I was a United States citizen, born in Brownsville, Texas. I was shipped off to a family that was not mine nor welcoming. I was told I had to go to school in the U.S. since I was a citizen here.

Imagine being a five-year-old kid without a mother or father. The house I grew up in with my cousins was an abusive hell. I felt like trash, unwanted, and always alone. I was homesick every day and cried real tears out of my heart. It was a nightly ritual for me. I hated being there and would've cut off my leg to be back in Matamoros.

One person who really helped me was my first-grade teacher, Mrs. Salinas. She took a special interest in me for some reason

A Government Secret

and always gave me extra attention. I didn't know how to read or write, which made me feel stupid. Mrs. Salinas gave me confidence and helped me learn it all. Without her, I would've been screwed.

She was so kind and gave me the motherly love I needed. Years later, she became one of my high school teachers. I was floored to see her and couldn't help but smile. She instantly recognized me. She recanted memories of me in first grade. I couldn't believe how sharp her mind was. She made my life and school much easier. She filled my emptiness and made me feel worthy. For this, I will always have admiration for Mrs. Salinas.

Some people came into my life and did amazing things for me. It's unreal how much love and compassion certain individuals have. After high school, I met different people on each new adventure. I went to work as a migrant worker. which was hard.

I remember going to Pasco, Washington, with my Uncle Kiko and friend Rene. We were promised a place to stay and work. After a few weeks, the owners wanted us to leave for some reason. There was still work, but we were singled out. Why? I have no idea. It left me totally up shit creek. No food, no place to stay. Rene knew some people from our hometown who were working nearby. I ended up meeting the men that would become my best friends in adult life. They took me in when I had nothing till I got back on my feet.

Ten of us lived in one trailer: Pepe, his wife, Elida, their two girls, Shayla & Karen, and Melia, Maqua, Kiko, Rene, Chute, and Javier. Elida would always make us tacos to take with us for lunch. I became great friends with Pepe, Chute, and Javier. They had such a huge influence on my life during my darkest times. They'll never truly know how much they saved my ass. I'll always be indebted to them for that.

Sadly, Pepe and Javier are no longer with us. Chute is the only one left out of those three. Javier stuck by me always. I never had a better friend than him and miss him daily. He's the reason I joined the military and went into law enforcement.

When this all began, I was a patriotic U.S. citizen who was willing to give the ultimate sacrifice for my country. I ended up finding out the hard way that my country, the U.S. did not feel the same for me. It took me finding out that I wasn't a U.S. citizen to learn this. This total experience has been a nightmare from hell for my entire family. When I'm asked by my kids, "Are you going to be deported, Dad?" I truly cannot answer that. I'm on a seesaw I can't seem to balance or get off.

Looking across the U.S. border wall into Mexico, a country that also said I was not a citizen thereof.

Through the heartache and totality of all this, I've met extraordinary people who have shown genuine love for us. They have consistently stuck out their necks for my family and me through the difficulties. Most of my new friends are fellow military brothers and sisters, people who understand the amount of sacrifice I've given to the U.S.

I've never been a law breaker, and I've lived my life on the straight and arrow. I've given everything, and yet I'm on the verge of being stripped of it all. I know nothing else but the U.S, the place where I planted my flag. Where I started a family and a career. Now I feel like I'm a wanderer with no home, no flag, and no status. All I ask is to be treated fairly.

I appreciate all who read my story. You be the judge. Do I deserve to be given U.S. citizenship or be deported? I just want to be draped in my U.S. flag. I fought so hard and served for many years. As of now, I have no flag to grasp onto. This has been unjustly stripped from me for a crime I never committed.

Is this the justice we are taught to believe in? You tell me.

Masters make the rules for the wise men and fools.

—Bob Dylan

Epilogue

Throughout this journey of life, I have met some of the best people out there. I believe God puts the right people in the right places. It's always a blessing to have wonderful friends in your life. I've lost many "good friends" after it was discovered I was not a U.S. citizen and fired from CBP. Those "friends" were fair-weather friends. You don't need those types in your life. Once a storm hits, they're the first to flee. With that being said, I hold zero animosity towards them.

One of my great friends is Frank Ramirez, whom I met in the sixth grade. We were like brothers almost. Clowning around with each other, beating the crap out of each other, and laughing about it a minute later. No holds barred. Nothing was sacred to us.. Insults by the truckload. If anyone else tried to be a part of our lingo, we'd take off on them instantly. Thanks for always being there, Frank.

Being in law enforcement, it's frowned upon to be around criminals or undocumented individuals. One guy who didn't give a shit about my status was Retired CBP Chief Warrant Officer John Garcia. *El Sombrerito*, the travelers called him. He's stayed by my side through it all. Thanks for being there for me, John.

a.k.a. "The JAG"

To my friend Daniel Nava, I appreciate the loyalty and friendship you've displayed for me and my family over the years. Danny has been a constant friend since we met years ago.

To Gil Vergara, who has never met me in person, reached out to me and my family. He knew I was a veteran in need. I cannot express enough thanks to you, Gil.

To Diana "Dee" Vega, former CEO of Repatriate our Patriots: Thank you for all you did for me and my family. Traveling down here to support us during my immigration proceedings and pointing me in the right direction. The resources you provided to me, which I wouldn't have known about, were invaluable to us.

To Diana "Dee" James, active CEO of Repatriate our Patriots: Thank you for being there for me. The moral and legal support, without ever asking for anything in return, has been priceless. Your friendship and assistance have brought tranquility during this crazy ordeal.

Thank you to All Relations United and especially my friend, CEO Loreli Horse Stands Waiting. Loreli, you have been a true, life-saving friend who's stood by me. You've been a great source of comfort and support throughout this process. I'm glad we finally were able to meet in person. I look foward to fighting the good fight on behalf of all veterans with you.

I cannot say thank you enough to all the veterans who have stuck by my side during this entire nightmare. You all have been my sounding board and understood my pain when I vented out. Your friendships have been pillars of strength that brought me solace.

Special thanks to Repatriate Our Patriots and All Relations United for their everlasting moral support. I appreciate your relentless battle and for not giving up on all deported veterans who need to come home.

Finally, I want to thank my family. To my beautiful wife, Anita, for being there through thick and thin. To my children, Daira, Raul, Artemio, and Mireya. Thank you for keeping me grounded and never giving up on me. Thank you for sticking with me through all this and showing me the humorous side of it. Without all of your love and support, this situation would have been much worse.